NB

Rights and Duties of Directors

Rights and Duties of Directors

Second edition

Desmond Wright, BA, FCA
Secretary to the Auditing Committee,
Institute of Chartered Accountants
in England and Wales

Brian Creighton, BSc, ACA
Senior Manager, Touche Ross & Co
Chartered Accountants

London, Dublin and Edinburgh
Butterworths
1991

United Kingdom	Butterworth & Co (Publishers) Ltd, 88 Kingsway, London WC2B 6AB and 4 Hill Street, Edinburgh EH2 3JZ
Australia	Butterworths Pty Ltd, Sydney, Melbourne, Brisbane, Adelaide, Perth, Canberra and Hobart
Canada	Butterworths Canada Ltd, Toronto and Vancouver
Ireland	Butterworths (Ireland) Ltd, Dublin
Malaysia	Malayan Law Journal Sdn Bhd, Kuala Lumpur
New Zealand	Butterworths of New Zealand Ltd, Wellington and Auckland
Puerto Rico	Equity de Puerto Rico, Inc, Hato Rey
Singapore	Malayan Law Journal Pte Ltd, Singapore
USA	Butterworths Legal Publishers, Austin, Texas; Boston, Massachusetts; Clearwater, Florida (D & S Publishers); Orford, New Hampshire (Equity Publishing); St Paul, Minnesota; and Seattle, Washington

A CIP Catalogue record for this book is available from the British Library.

First edition 1987

ISBN 0 406 67846 4

Typeset by Butler & Tanner Ltd
Printed and bound in Great Britain by
Butler & Tanner Ltd, Frome and London

Preface

The main reason for updating the first edition of this book was the arrival of the Companies Act 1989. In addition to implementing the Seventh EC Directive on Group Accounts the 1989 Act amended and added to the Companies Act 1985 in various areas. For example, listed companies may now issue summary financial statements, private companies may use elective and written resolutions to relieve some of the administrative burdens placed upon them by legislation and all companies are subject to the defective accounts procedures.

The update also gave the opportunity to include a number of legal cases that shed light on the provisions of the Insolvency Act 1986, the Company Directors Disqualification Act 1986 and other legislation.

I am indebted to the various people within Touche Ross who helped in the revision of this book. In particular I would like to thank Ken Wild and Hayden Everitt of Touche Ross and Jennifer James LLB, BCL, Senior Lecturer at Reading University for their comments on an earlier draft.

I am grateful for permission to refer in the text to the following publications: *Palmer's Company Law* (24th edn) by C M Schmitthoff and others, published by Stevens & Sons; *The Admission of Securities to Listing* published by the Council of The Stock Exchange; and *Guidelines for Directors, Directors' Personal Liabilities* and *Insider Dealing* published by the Institute of Directors.

All statutory references are to the Companies Act 1985 (as revised) unless otherwise indicated. The law is stated as at 24 June 1991, the date on which Commencement Order No 11 to the Companies Act 1989 was made.

August 1991 Brian Creighton

In order to be of the widest possible use, this book has been written in general terms. Its application to specific situations will depend upon the particular circumstances involved. Accordingly, it is recommended that the reader seeks proper professional advice regarding any particular problems that he encounters, and this book should not be relied on as a substitute for such advice. While all reasonable care has been taken in the preparation of this book, no responsibility is accepted by the authors, Touche Ross or the publisher for any errors it may contain, whether caused by negligence or otherwise, or for any loss, howsoever caused, occasioned to any person by reliance on it.

Preface to first edition

A company director who does not meet the high standards of conduct required by the law can be subject to a formidable array of liabilities and penalties. This concise but comprehensive guide to his legal responsibilities will help him keep both his company and himself out of trouble. I hope that the information and practical advice it contains will be of value to all directors, regardless of their knowledge and experience. However, it should be of particular interest to directors of 'family' companies, to their professional advisers and to non-executive directors.

I have tried to devise a structure which caters both for the reader who is completely new to the field and at the same time for the reader who has a reasonable level of non-specialist knowledge. Each chapter has a detailed list of contents followed by a simplified view, in italics, of the major principles. The main text then amplifies and explains these principles, indicating qualifications and taking the discussion to a level that should interest the non-specialist lawyer or accountant. I have used legal terms, where appropriate, but I have tried to make their meaning clear by context. For those still lost, I have provided a glossary explaining many of the terms that recur throughout the book. I have given full references to statutes, case law and other authorities, to provide avenues for further research. Wherever possible I have attempted to give practical guidance in response to the legal requirements.

One advantage of writing a book from within a large international firm of chartered accountants is the almost unlimited range of specialised knowledge and expertise available to the author. I hope, therefore, that the many people within Touche Ross who helped me in so many ways will understand if I single out Ken Wild, partner in charge of accounting research: if it were not for his help and encouragement, this book would not have been written. I would also like to thank Brenda Hannigan BA, MA, TCD, LLM, solicitor and member of the Faculty of Law at Southampton University, for her valuable comments on an early draft.

November 1986

Desmond Wright
Secretary to the Auditing Committee
and formerly Senior Manager,
Touche Ross & Co

Contents

Table of statutes

Table of cases

References

Throughout this book, unless otherwise specified, the statutory references are to the Companies Act 1985 (as amended). References to articles are to Table A of the Companies (Tables A to F) Regulations 1985.

Introduction to the company

A company is legally a person with an identity entirely separate from that of its members, with the capacity to undertake many of the commercial activities carried on by living people. It functions within a legal framework of statute – principally the Companies Act 1985 – and common law. Subject to these constraints, the company's activities are governed by its memorandum and articles of association.

The company's memorandum regulates its relations with the outside world, setting out its name, domicile, objects, limitation of liability and authorised share capital. The objects clause of the memorandum is important because it defines what acts are intra vires *– within the power of – the company. Acts not within the scope of the objects clause are* ultra vires *and may not be legally valid.*

The articles set out the internal regulations of the company. Unless specifically modified or excluded, specimen articles set out in Table A of the Companies Act apply. Companies which adopt Table A adopt the version in force at the date of their incorporation: any subsequent changes to the Table do not automatically apply and must be adopted specifically if required.

Most companies are limited by shares: that is, the liability of the individual members for the debts of the company is limited to the nominal value of the share capital for which they have applied. A company limited by shares must not issue shares beyond the amount authorised in its memorandum. This is expressed as a nominal amount of share capital divided into a number of shares of a fixed amount. Shareholders do not necessarily have to pay the full price at once and may await calls from the company. However, in practice, the allotted share capital of most companies is fully paid. If the shares are issued at a price in excess of their nominal value the excess is called the share premium and must for most purposes be treated by the company as if it were share capital.

There can be various classes of shares. The ones most commonly encountered are preference shares, which give holders preferential rights to dividends or assets or both, and ordinary shares (sometimes called equity shares) which confer on holders the residual rights which have not been conferred on other classes of shares.

Companies can also be formed without a share capital, the members' liability in such cases being limited to specific amounts guaranteed in the event of a winding up. Since 1980 it has not been possible to form or to become a company limited by guarantee with a share capital (section 1) but such companies, formed before 1980, still operate. There are also unlimited companies, in which the members accept unlimited liability for the company's debts. Such companies are rare but enjoy the privilege of not having to file annual accounts.

The company's life begins when the promoters submit the required documents – including the memorandum, articles and a statement of the directors and company secretary – to the registrar of companies and receive a certificate of incorporation. The company must maintain a registered office at which legal documents can be served.

A limited company can be either public or private. Public limited companies (plcs) must meet certain minimum requirements as to share capital and are subject to a range of other restrictions not applied to private companies. Their major advantage is that they can offer their shares to the public and thus raise capital on, for example, The Stock Exchange. Private companies are otherwise more flexible and are much more common.

Every company must have at least two members, who own shares and have the right to vote at general meetings. The principal instrument of the general meeting is the members' resolution, which can be an ordinary resolution requiring a simple majority, a special resolution requiring a 75% majority or an elective resolution requiring unanimous consent. Special resolutions are required under the Act in order to carry out certain actions (such as a change in the objects clause) and may be required in other circumstances laid down in the articles. Prior to the Companies Act 1989 all companies were required to hold an annual general meeting of members each year – but the 1989 Act allows private companies to dispense with the requirement by elective resolution. A company may in addition hold extraordinary general meetings. The powers of the general meeting are laid down in the company's articles. Usually management of the company's affairs is vested in the board of directors rather than the members in general meeting.

A private company must have at least one director and a public company at least two. Subject to the overriding provisions of the Companies Act, the articles set out the precise powers and duties of the directors, usually entrusting them with management of the company. In general law the directors do not have the power to act individually on behalf of the company and must act collectively as a board. However, the articles usually allow the board to confer individual management authority on the managing director and to delegate other duties to executive directors as it thinks fit.

1 The nature of office

1.50 Types of director

1.51 Alternate directors
1.52 Associate directors
1.53 Executive directors
1.54 Non-executive directors
1.55 Permanent directors
1.56 Managing director
1.57 Nominee directors

It is well established law that you cannot hang a company's common seal (R v City of London (1692) Skin 310). *Although a company is a separate legal person it is obviously incapable of acting on its own behalf and can operate only through its directors and other officers with the appropriate authority. What then, is the status of these directors, who are they and how are they appointed?*

When acting for the company a director legally binds it as if he were its agent. Since he is also responsible for the company's assets he has also been described as a trustee. However, neither of these analogies is strictly accurate and the most that can be said is that a director occupies a position akin to that of both an agent and a trustee. He may also – although not necessarily – be an employee of the company.

Virtually all questions relating to the eligibility and appointment of directors are decided by reference to the articles of association. The Companies Act is almost entirely silent on these matters, leaving whoever sets up the company a free hand to establish its rules. However, certain people are disqualified by law from acting as directors, principally bankrupts or anyone declared unfit by the courts on the basis of previous conduct in relation to companies.

Most companies require directors to be elected by the members – although this is again dependent on the articles. On the other hand the articles cannot set aside the right of members under the Companies Act to remove a director by a simple majority.

1.10 WHO IS A DIRECTOR?

Who indeed? The Act does not define a director, although section 741 (1) provides that the term includes 'any person occupying the position of director, by whatever name called'. Thus a director is recognised not by his title but by his function, which depends on the nature of the company, the provisions of its articles and the contents of the director's service contract – if he has one. A company may describe its directors as, for example, 'governors', 'trustees' or 'council members' without affecting their legal status as directors.

Unfortunately, the reverse is also true. It is not uncommon for a company to bestow the title 'director' on an individual who does not sit on the board. According to the Institute of Directors, if such a person is 'held out to the outside world with the title of "director", without qualification, they cannot expect wholly to escape the responsibilities which go with that office' (*Guidelines for Directors 1990,* paragraph 87). Some of the legal implications of persons being held out as having the authority of directors are dealt with in paragraph 2.23, below. See also associate directors in paragraph 1.52, below.

1.11 Shadow director

A shadow director is 'a person in accordance with whose directions or instructions the directors of the company are accustomed to act' unless they act only on his professional advice (section 741(2)). He is thus a person who has the powers of a director without being formally appointed, and the Act specifies that many of the statutory duties owed by directors are also owed by shadow directors, particularly in the sections relating to the enforcement of fair dealings. Shadow directors are also caught by the wrongful trading provisions of the Insolvency Act 1986 (see paragraph 11.23, below) and the unfitness provisions of the Company Directors Disqualification Act 1986 (see paragraph 1.33, below).

A banker or other lender who controls the actions of the directors, even for legitimate commercial reasons, may be a shadow director (*Re a Company* (*No 005009 of 1987*) (1988) 4 BCC 424). So may a company, as in the case of a holding company.

It is likely that a shadow director is anyway a 'person occupying the position of director' and therefore a director under section 741.

1.12 The director as agent

The articles usually provide for the company's business to be managed by the board, so that the acts of the directors become the acts of the company. The relationship takes on a number of the legal characteristics of agent and principal, the most important being that when a director enters into a contract within his authority he binds the company without necessarily becoming personally liable.

However, there are peculiarities in the relationship between director and company which strain the analogy with agency. As was pointed out in *Northern Counties Securities Ltd v Jackson and Steeple Ltd* [1974] 2 All ER 625, the director 'is an agent who casts his vote to decide in what manner his principal shall act'. With his co-directors a director controls the activities of his company, so his powers are greater than those normally accorded an agent.

Accordingly, company law has evolved various provisions to account for the special position of directors. For example, if a director signs a cheque which is not in the full name of the company he becomes personally liable if the company defaults (section 349). The company can, of course, honour the cheque. Similarly, if a director enters into a contract outside his authority he may become liable, but the company can ratify the contract and take the benefit. These matters are discussed in more detail in Chapter 2.

1.13 The director as trustee

If directors are the agents of the company in the transactions which they enter into on its behalf, they are also trustees of company assets under their control. However, the true nature of a trust would be to vest ownership of the assets in the directors themselves. This does not occur with a company because, as a legal person, it owns property in its own right.

Directors are trustees only insofar as they owe a duty of good faith to the company. However, although this duty is similar to the fiduciary duty owed by trustees it is different in that, for example, directors must take risks when managing the company which would not be permitted by a trustee. Similarly, the director's duty of skill and care is less demanding than that required of a trustee.

1.14 The director as employee

There is nothing to preclude a director from also being an employee. In the case, for example, of *Lee v Lee's Air Farming Ltd* [1961] AC 12 the managing director was also the pilot of the company's only plane and held to be acting in the dual capacities of director and employee.

However, a director is not an employee by virtue of his directorship. Whether he is also an employee is a matter of fact, evidenced by the existence of a contract of employment. This need not be written, but the courts have sometimes been reluctant to infer a contract of employment merely from the conduct of the parties. In the case of

Parsons v Albert J Parsons & Sons Ltd [1979] ICR 271 there was no express contract either oral or written; the court held that a director was not an employee even though he worked full-time in the business.

The importance of the principle of dual capacity is that the director when acting as an employee will have an additional and a completely separate set of rights and duties. For example, if he is dismissed as a director he is not necessarily dismissed as an employee and he will have rights under employment protection legislation. On the other hand, the level of skill he is required to display in dealing with the company's affairs as an employee may be higher than that as a director. These considerations are dealt with more fully as they occur throughout the book.

1.20 ELIGIBILITY AND APPOINTMENT

1.21 Number of directors

Section 282 provides that every private company must have at least one director and every public company at least two. The articles may prescribe a higher minimum number, or a maximum (although there is no statutory limit).

1.22 Who can be a director?

Although certain categories of person are disqualified from acting as a director (see paragraph 1.31, below), the Act does not lay down any specific qualification for office. Subject to the articles, therefore, the following are all capable of being appointed directors:

(a) a minor;

(b) a person of unsound mind (this is not allowed under Table A);

(c) an alien;

(d) another company.

The articles can impose any qualification as a prerequisite for holding office. Such a qualification requirement may be an effective way of limiting members' power of appointment, since a simple majority usually suffices to appoint a director but a 75% majority is required to change the articles.

1.23 Qualification shares

A common qualification laid down in the articles is for a director to hold a certain number of shares in the company. However, Table A does not lay down any such requirement. Prior to 1985, article 77 merely provided that 'the shareholding qualification for directors may be fixed by the company in general meeting, and unless and until so fixed no qualification shall be required'. This regulation was omitted when Table A was revised in 1985.

However, if the articles do impose a share qualification section 291 imposes a number of rules:

(a) The qualification shares must be obtained within two months of appointment (or a shorter time specified in the articles). If the articles specify that a person must hold the qualification shares before he is eligible to become a director, the period of grace does not apply and a purported appointment is void (*Jenner's* case (1877) 7 Ch D 132).

(b) Share warrants do not constitute shares for this purpose.

(c) A director who fails to acquire his qualification shares in time, or who ceases to hold them, automatically vacates his office, and is liable to a default fine if he continues to act as a director. However, an increase in the qualification shareholding does not automatically disqualify the director (*Molineaux v London, Birmingham and Manchester Insurance Co Ltd* [1902] 2 KB 589).

In practice, qualification shareholdings are relatively rare today. However, their former prevalence has produced plenty of case law. The following indicate what holdings can constitute qualification shares:

(a) A joint holding qualifies a director (*Grundy v Biggs* [1901] 1 Ch 444) unless the articles provide otherwise.

(b) A trustee shareholding qualifies even if the articles specify a holding 'in his own right', since it has been held that the test of shareholding is entry in the register of members, not whether there is a beneficial interest in the shares (for example, *Bainbridge v Smith* (1889) 41 Ch D 462).

(c) However, the company must be able to safely deal with the director as the owner of the shares. Thus in *Sutton v English and Colonial Produce Co Ltd* [1902] 2 Ch 502 where the director was bankrupt, the court held that he could not be said to hold the shares in his own right.

(d) A representative holding, for example as executor or liquidator, does not qualify if entered as such in the register (*Boschoek Pty Co Ltd v Fuke* [1906] 1 Ch 148).

Qualification shares may be obtained from any source. However, the shares cannot normally be given by the company or bought with a loan from the company, because of the general prohibition on a company giving financial assistance for the acquisition of its shares (section 151).

1.24 Appointment of first directors

Section 10 requires the subscribers, when delivering the memorandum to the registrar, to deliver also a statement of, amongst other things, the names of the first directors. (Following the practice of numbering the prescribed form according to the section to which it relates, this statement is on Form 10.) The statement must also be signed by anyone named as a director indicating consent to act. Thus, in practice, the first directors are usually appointed by the subscribers to the memorandum. A purported appointment by any other means – for example, by naming the directors in the articles – is void unless the same directors are named on Form 10.

1.25 Subsequent appointments

Many companies adopt article 73 of Table A, which requires all the directors to retire at the first annual general meeting. At subsequent annual general meetings one-third of the directors retire by rotation, determined by length of service since appointment or reappointment. If directors have the same length of service, retirement is determined by lot or by some other method agreed among themselves (article 74). A retiring director is eligible for re-election, and under article

75 he is deemed to be reappointed unless the meeting votes not to fill the vacancy or a motion to reappoint him is defeated.

It will be necessary to check the articles of a private company that wishes to dispense with holding an annual general meeting (see paragraph 7.30, below); in case the articles require certain acts to be authorised at the annual general meeting (eg as discussed in this paragraph and paragraph 1.26, below).

The articles may allow a director to assign his office, but any assignment must be approved by special resolution (section 308).

1.26 Casual vacancies

Under Table A, existing directors have a general power to fill a vacancy or to appoint an additional director subject to any limitation in the articles as to maximum number. Anyone filling a casual vacancy holds office only until the next annual general meeting, when he must retire and, if appropriate, offer himself for re-election. He is not counted among the directors retiring by rotation and, unlike them, vacates office at the conclusion of the meeting unless he is specifically re-elected (article 79). Listed companies are required to include a provision in their articles that the filler of a casual vacancy holds office only until the next annual general meeting (*Admission of Securities to Listing* section 9, Chapter 1, paragraph 4.2).

Any new director must sign a consent to act in that capacity which must be lodged with the registrar (section 288).

1.27 Restrictions on the members' right to appoint

Although the members are always entitled to remove a director by ordinary resolution (section 303, see paragraph 1.42, below), they have no statutory right of appointment. For example, the articles may give the directors alone the power to add to their number. However, the courts are reluctant to recognise a provision which takes the right of appointment away from members unless it is totally unambiguous (for example, *Worcester Corsetry Ltd v Witting* [1936] Ch 640).

If the articles provide for directors to be appointed by the company in general meeting, section 292 imposes the Act's only requirement in this area: directors of a public company must be elected individually unless there has been unanimous agreement to appoint two or more together. This allows shareholders to reject a particular director without rejecting the whole board. Table A gives members a right to appoint a new director subject to certain procedural rules. Article 76 provides that only a director retiring by rotation or a person recommended by the directors can be proposed at a general meeting unless written notice has been given. The notice must be signed by a member entitled to vote at the meeting, and must be accompanied by a notice from the candidate of his willingness to be appointed.

The time limit for lodging the notice varies. Article 76 provides that it must be given to the company not less than 14 nor more than 35 clear days before the date of the meeting. However, the version of Table A in force before 1 July 1985 specified not less than three nor more than 21 days (article 93), and this will still be included in many companies' articles. Listed companies must ensure their articles comply with the Yellow Book requirement that the minimum period during which lodgement can be made is seven days, and the latest date for lodgement must be not more than seven days before the meeting (*Admission of Securities to Listing* section 9, Chapter 1, paragraphs 4.4, 4.5).

The notice must include the same information about the candidate as is required for the register of directors (see paragraph 4.51, below).

1.30 DISQUALIFICATION

The Insolvency Act 1985 introduced a number of new grounds on which directors could be disqualified by the court. These provisions were subsequently consolidated with the existing provisions of the Companies Act in the Company Directors Disqualification Act 1986.

Official statistics indicate that there were 309 directors disqualification orders in 1990, compared with 303 in 1989, 322 in 1988 and 159 in 1987.

1.31 Disqualification orders

A disqualification order made by the court prohibits an individual not only from acting as a director, but also from acting as a liquidator, or as a receiver or manager of the company's property, and from having any connection with the setting up or management of a company (Company Directors Disqualification Act 1986, section 1). However, the court has discretion to allow an individual to act while disqualified. This means that a director can be given a limited period in which to hand over his responsibilities (*Re Ipcon Fashions Ltd* (1989) 5 BCC 773) or even be given leave to take part in the management of a particular company subject to certain conditions (*Re Lo-Line Electric Motors Ltd* (1988) 4 BCC 415; *Re Majestic Recording Studios Limited* (1988) 4 BCC 519, *Re Chartmore Ltd* [1990] BCLC 673).

In *Chartmore* the disqualified director was allowed to remain director of a new company subject to certain conditions, including a requirement to hold proper monthly board meetings attended by a representative of the auditors.

1.32 General misconduct in connection with companies

There are four categories of general misconduct for which the court may issue a disqualification order against a director:

(a) Conviction of an indictable offence committed in connection with the setting up, management or liquidation of a company, or with the receivership or management of its property (Company Directors Disqualification Act 1986, section 2). It appears from *R v Georgiou* (1988) 4 BCC 322 that the phrase 'in connection with management' is to be widely construed. The maximum period of disqualification under this head is five years if imposed by a magistrates' court or 15 years otherwise.

(b) Persistent breaches of the Companies Act requirement to file returns, accounts or other documents with, or to give notice to, the registrar (Company Directors Disqualification Act 1986, section 3). (What constitutes 'persistent' is considered below.) The maximum period of disqualification that can be imposed by any court under this head is five years.

(c) Fraudulent trading (see paragraph 11.22, below) or fraud against the company discovered in the course of a winding up (Company Directors Disqualification Act 1986, section 4). The maximum period of disqualification under this head is 15 years.

(d) Summary conviction of an offence relating to the Companies Act requirements to file returns, accounts or other documents (Company Directors Disqualification Act 1986, section 5). The maximum period of disqualification under this head is five years.

An application to a court for a disqualification order against a person for general misconduct may be made by any past or present member or creditor of any company in relation to which the person has committed or is alleged to have committed an offence or other default (Company Directors Disqualification Act 1986, section 16).

Persistent default in relation to the filing requirements may be conclusively proved by showing that a person has been adjudged guilty of three or more defaults in the previous five years (Company Directors Disqualification Act, section 3). He is adjudged guilty if he has been convicted of any offence consisting in a contravention of or a failure to comply with the filing or notice provisions, or if a default order is made against him. Default orders can be made by the court against directors to enforce delivery of the company's accounts (section 242) or to enforce the company's duty to make other statutory returns (section 713). Any member or creditor, or the registrar may apply to the court for such a default order. Default orders may also be made by the court to enforce directors to prepare revised accounts (section 245B, see paragraph 5.66, below). Persistent default may also be proved in any other way.

1.33 Unfitness

The Insolvency Act 1985 significantly increased the risk to a director of being disqualified as unfit to be involved in the management of a company. It did this principally by extending the circumstances in which an individual might be disqualified, by setting out the matters to be particularly taken into account by the court when determining unfitness, and by requiring insolvency practitioners to investigate the conduct of directors prior to a company's insolvency.

There are two circumstances in which an individual may be disqualified for unfitness. (The grounds on which he may be found unfit are considered below.) The maximum period of disqualification is 15 years.

(a) The court has a duty to disqualify a director for a minimum of two years if it is satisfied that his conduct in relation to an insolvent company (see paragraph 11.14, below) makes him unfit to be concerned with the management of a company (Company Directors Disqualification Act 1986, section 6). Application for a disqualification order on this ground may be made by the Secretary of State if it appears to him to be in the public interest (or by the official receiver if so directed by the Secretary of State) (Company Directors Disqualification Act 1986, section 7).

(b) The Secretary of State may apply for a disqualification order if, after an investigation under the Companies Act 1985 or the Financial Services Act 1986 (see paragraphs 4.71, 4.72 and 4.74, below) an order appears to him to be expedient in the public interest. The court may then make an order if satisfied that an individual's conduct renders him unfit (Company Directors Disqualification Act 1986, section 8).

The unfitness provisions also apply specifically to shadow directors (Company Directors Disqualification Act 1986, section 22).

Schedule 1 of the Company Directors Disqualification Act 1986 lists the matters to which the court is to have particular regard in determining whether a director is unfit for office and therefore liable to disqualification. This list is not meant to restrict the matters to be considered by the court and is not an exhaustive list of a director's duties under the Companies Act 1985 (*Re Bath Glass Ltd* (1987) 4 BCC 130). The following apply irrespective of whether the company is insolvent:

(a) misfeasance or breach of duty to the company;

(b) misapplication of the company's money or property, or any conduct giving rise to an obligation to account to the company for money or property (for example, a secret profit, see paragraph 3.24, below);

(c) responsibility for transactions defrauding creditors (see paragraph 11.33, below);

(d) responsibility for the company's failure to:

  (i) keep accounting records and retain them for the prescribed period;

(ii) maintain the register of directors and secretaries;

(iii) maintain a register of members and keep it in the prescribed location;

(iv) make an annual return within the prescribed period;

(v) register charges on the company's assets;

(e) responsibility for the failure of the directors of the company to prepare signed annual accounts.

If the company is insolvent, a director may be adjudged unfit depending on the extent of his responsibility for the following:

(a) the insolvency of the company;

(b) any failure to supply a customer who has paid in advance;

(c) any voidable transaction or preference (see paragraph 11.30 ff, below);

(d) any failure to comply with the requirements relating to the first meeting of creditors in a voluntary winding up;

(e) any failure to comply with an obligation relating to a statement of affairs in a winding up;

(f) the failure of anyone holding company property to deliver it up;

(g) any failure in a duty to co-operate with a liquidator.

Insolvency practitioners must report any examples of unfit conduct which come to their attention (Company Directors Disqualification Act 1986, section 7). They are required to render reports on all directors who held office in the three years prior to insolvency (Insolvent Companies (Reports on Conduct of Directors) No 2 Rules 1986, rule 4).

Re Sevenoaks Stationers (Retail) Ltd [1990] BCC 765 provided the first appeal for a disqualification order under this section. In this case it was held that incompetence or negligence to a 'very marked degree' is enough to render a director unfit, a director should know which charges he had to meet, a director could not be disqualified on the basis of charges that were not made against him and that non-payment of crown debts was not automatic evidence of unfitness.

1.34 Other cases of disqualification

An individual also faces disqualification in the following circumstances:

(a) if he has been found liable for fraudulent or wrongful trading under sections 213 or 214 of the Insolvency Act 1986 (see paragraphs 11.22 and 11.23, below), he may be disqualified by court order for up to 15 years without further application (Company Directors Disqualification Act 1986, section 10);

(b) if he is an undischarged bankrupt he is automatically disqualified, unless the court's permission is obtained. On receiving an application for permission, the court must notify the official receiver, who has a duty to oppose the application if he believes the public interest is threatened (Company Directors Disqualification Act 1986, section 11); or

(c) under the County Courts Act 1984 a county court may, as an alternative to bankruptcy, make an administration order in relation to a debtor's affairs. (This should not be confused with an administration order made on a company under the Insolvency Act.) Such an order will require regular payments by the debtor. If the debtor fails to make a payment the court may revoke the order and make an order imposing on the debtor some of the disabilities of an undischarged bankrupt. Except with the leave of the court, the debtor may not act as director of a company or take part directly or indirectly in its management (Company Directors Disqualification Act 1986, section 12). Contravention of such an order is an offence but does not render the debtor personally liable for a company's debts. Nor does the prohibition extend to those acting on the debtor's instructions. The order is for a maximum of two years.

1.35 Penalties

It is a criminal offence to act as a director while disqualified, with a maximum punishment of two years' imprisonment and a fine (Company Directors Disqualification Act 1986, section 13). In addition, if a person involves himself in the management of a company while disqualified he becomes jointly and severally liable (with the company and anyone else similarly liable) for the relevant debts of the company. Anyone who manages the company subject to the instructions of a disqualified person is also personally liable (Company Directors Disqualification Act 1986, section 15).

1.36 Statutory ineligibility

The following are precluded from holding office as a director:

(a) The auditor of the company or of any company in the same group cannot be an officer (eg director or company secretary) or employee of the company (Companies Act 1989, section 27).

(b) The company secretary cannot be the sole director of a company (section 283).

1.37 Vacation of office under the articles

The articles may include any provision for disqualifying a director from office. Article 81 specifies, in addition to the statutory prohibitions, three other occasions on which a director vacates his office:

(a) if he becomes a bankrupt or makes any arrangement or composition with his creditors generally (this is more extensive than the disqualification of bankrupts under section 11 of the Company Directors Disqualification Act 1986);

(b) if he suffers from a mental disorder and is either admitted to hospital under the Mental Health Acts or becomes the subject of a court order;

(c) if he is absent from directors' meetings for more than six consecutive months and the board resolves that he should vacate his office.

Note that in the case of prolonged absence the director does not vacate his office unless this is confirmed by the board. However, he vacates his office automatically on the occurrence of either of the other events (*Re Bodega Co Ltd* [1904] 1 Ch 276).

1.38 The 70 year age limit

Section 293 broadly prohibits a person who has reached the age of 70 from acting as a director of a public company or one of its subsidiaries. However:

(a) the director may be elected or re-elected after reaching the age of 70 provided his appointment is approved by the members in general meeting and 28 days' notice has been given of the resolution to appoint him;

(b) the articles may exclude the provisions of this section altogether, or substitute some different age limit.

A person who has reached retirement age and is appointed or proposed to be appointed to a public company or its subsidiary has a duty under section 294 to give notice of his age to the company. This does not apply to an existing director, whose age will already be disclosed in the register of directors (see paragraph 4.51, below).

1.40 RESIGNATION AND REMOVAL

1.41 Resignation

It is always open to a director to resign, although the articles may impose restrictions or conditions. Article 81 allows a director to resign by giving notice to the company. It then becomes immediately effective and cannot be withdrawn, even if it has not been formally accepted (*Glossop v Glossop* [1907] 2 Ch 370). Prior to 1 July 1985, Table A required notice in writing, but *Latchford Premier Cinema Ltd v Ennion* [1931] 2 Ch 409 had already established that a director would be bound by an oral resignation given and accepted at a general meeting.

The director's right to resign does not free him from any obligations under his service contract, which may give the company the opportunity to sue for damages.

1.42 Dismissal by members' ordinary resolution

'A company may by ordinary resolution remove a director before the expiration of his period of office, notwithstanding anything in its articles or in any agreement between it and him.' Section 303 thus gives members an absolute right to remove a director by a simple majority (ordinary resolution) at any time.

A resolution under this section requires 28 days' notice to the company. On receipt of such notice the company must notify the director concerned, who has a right to be heard at the meeting. The director also has a right to have his written representations circulated to members by the company, unless the court is satisfied that this right is being abused to secure needless publicity for defamatory matter (section 304).

Although section 303 is an important element in the machinery of shareholder control, the power it confers is by no means untrammelled. The following are the major weapons available for the director's defence.

(a) He can pursue a claim for compensation under a service contract. However, as such a contract cannot exceed five years unless approved by the members in general meeting (section 319, see paragraph 9.20, below), it is difficult for directors to make their dismissal prohibitively expensive.

(b) He can petition the court for a just and equitable winding up under section 122 of the Insolvency Act 1986. Such a course was successfully pursued in *Ebrahim's v Westbourne Galleries Ltd* [1973] AC 360. The House of Lords held that a director with a substantial stake in a small private company 'formed on a basis of personal relationship involving mutual confidence' was owed a duty of good faith by his fellow directors. His removal was held to have removed the basis on which the company was incorporated, that of mutual participation in management by the shareholders. Although the court did not reject the company's right to remove the director, it granted a petition for winding up. Such considerations are said to apply to 'quasi partnerships' and may not be available in public companies.

(c) It is possible for the company to adopt an article conferring weighted voting rights on a director in the event of a resolution to remove him from office. In *Bushell v Faith* [1970] AC 1099 such an article was held to be valid and not an infringement of section 303. In this case the company's 300 shares were divided equally among the three directors with an article increasing a threatened directors' voting rights to three votes per share. Thus two directors voting to remove the third would be outvoted, and would not be able to muster the 75% majority required to change the article.

1.43 Dismissal by the board

The board has no power to remove a director unless the articles specifically confer such a power (*Hayes v Bristol Plant Hire Ltd* [1957] 1 All ER 685). Although Table A contains no such provision it is relatively common, particularly in the articles of public companies where it enables boardroom disputes to be settled out of the public eye. There is a discussion in paragraph 8.20, below, of the steps available to a director who disagrees with the rest of the board.

1.50 TYPES OF DIRECTOR

1.51 Alternate directors

An alternate director is a person appointed by a director to speak and act on his behalf. Most company articles, including the 1985 version of Table A, allow alternate directors.

Under article 65 any director is entitled to appoint another director, or any other person approved by the board, to act as his alternate. The alternate is entitled 'to perform all the functions of his appointor as a director in his absence' but is not entitled to any remuneration from the company (article 66).

An alternate 'is deemed for all purposes to be a director' and acts on his own account, not as agent for his appointor (article 69).

1.52 Associate directors

The term associate director has no particular standing in law, and is used generically to include assistant, divisional, regional and special directors, who are normally senior executives without a seat on the board. There are dangers attached to conferring such titles on people who do not have the powers and duties of directors.

(a) The individual may be held to be 'occupying the position of director' and thus a *de facto* director under section 741. He would thus run the risk of being held liable for breaches of duties he was unaware of.

(b) If he is held out as being a director he may have the power to bind the company in contracts outside his actual authority (see paragraph 2.20 ff, below).

1.53 Executive directors

Executive directors carry out executive functions in the company, usually under contracts of employment, in addition to their board duties. The usual examples are the managing director or the chief executive, to whom the board delegates its management powers. Some companies use the term executive director to denote someone with the status of an associate director, but fortunately this usage is rare.

1.54 Non-executive directors

Non-executive directors are not employees of the company and usually serve only part-time. Their fiduciary duty to the company is identical to that of executive directors, although their duty of skill and care may be less demanding (see Chapter 3). They participate fully in the joint deliberations of the board but do not have any executive function in the company's management.

1.55 Permanent directors

The articles may provide for permanent directors who do not have to submit themselves for periodic re-election. Such directors can, however, be removed under section 303.

1.56 Managing director

The articles usually enable the board to delegate any or all of its powers of management to one or more of their number. A managing director does not retire by rotation (article 84).

1.57 Nominee directors

A nominee director is usually appointed to satisfy a major shareholder or the company's bankers. However, according to Lord Denning a nominee director must be left free to exercise his best judgement in the interests of the company, and not merely to follow the directions of his patron (*Boulting v Association of Cinematograph, Television and Allied Technicians* [1963] 2 QB 606). Thus he has the same duties to the company as any other director.

2 The directors' powers

Just as you cannot hang a company, so there are limits to what a company itself can do. For example, it cannot get married. Apart from such inherent limitations, the limits of a company's powers are defined in its constitution, principally in its memorandum. Normally the company acts through its directors, whose powers are accordingly limited to those the company itself has under its constitution. The company's constitution may further limit the powers of all or some of the directors, or establish procedures that must be followed before the directors can bind the company.

In practice the articles usually give the directors full authority to manage the company's business and to exercise all its powers subject to the Act, the memorandum and articles and special resolutions. The board can then in turn delegate its functions to individual directors. However, if there are limitations they do not necessarily prevent the company from being bound when a director exceeds his or the company's powers. Third parties contracting with the company are protected against a director exceeding his authority in the following circumstances:

- *Where a third party deals with the company in good faith, any transaction decided on by the directors is within the directors' capacity (section 35A).*

- *Where a director has apparent authority to act on the company's behalf (because he is, for example, the managing director or is held out by the company as having the authority) the company must abide by the contract (see paragraph 2.23, below).*

- *The acts of a director or manager are valid even if there is a defect in his appointment (section 285).*

Also, in certain circumstances, a third party can claim against the director. This applies principally when either the director does not indicate he is acting on behalf of the company, or he suggests in some way that he has authority when in fact he does not (see paragraph 2.30, below).

As a legal person a company can not only enter into valid contracts, it can also commit a variety of civil and criminal offences. Clearly those offences must be initiated and carried out by the company's human agents, who are generally personally liable for their actions. However, directors who do not participate in or connive at an offence cannot generally be held liable. Often the company itself is liable, but the considerations, particularly in relation to civil liability, are complex.

2.10 SOURCES OF DIRECTORS' POWERS

2.11 Powers of the company

A company has a legal personality only by virtue of its constitution, and can accordingly act only within the powers given to it by its constitution. This means that it must act within the objects clause of its memorandum and in accordance with the rules of management established by its articles. If a company acts outside the objects for which it is incorporated its action may be *ultra vires* and void. (A void transaction is treated as if it had never taken place and any assets that have changed hands must be returned.)

The Companies Act 1989 has made fundamental changes in this area which are intended to give general relief from the effects of the *ultra vires* doctrine, while maintaining it internally as a limit to the powers of the directors (see paragraph 2.21, below).

This relief does not apply to *ultra vires* transactions with directors of the company or persons connected with them. Such transactions are voidable by the company (section 322A, see paragraph 2.22, below). Also the relief is restricted by section 30B(1) of the Charities Act 1960 and section 112(3) of the Companies Act 1989 in relation to companies that are charities.

Another of the changes made by the Companies Act 1989 allows a company to include in its objects clause a statement that it will carry on business as a general commercial company. This will enable the company to carry on any trade or business whatsoever and to do anything that is incidental or conducive to that trade or business.

Such a clause precludes the need for a widely drafted objects clause, a practice that has been increasingly common in recent years as it permitted a company to engage legally in any activity it might conceivably want to.

2.12 Exercise of the company's powers

The Companies Act does not set out which actions are within the directors' power, although it frequently imposes restrictions. It is the articles which, in allocating the powers the company itself has under its constitution, define the directors' authority.

Article 70 of Table A states that 'the business of the company shall be managed by the directors who may exercise all the powers of the company' but this is 'subject to the provisions of the Act, the memorandum and the articles and to any directions given by special resolution'. Under these provisions, therefore, the members have the right to dictate to the board by means of special resolution. Many companies do not have such a provision in their articles, in which case, once the articles have given the directors power to manage the company, the members cannot interfere (*Automatic Self-Cleansing Filter Syndicate Co Ltd v Cuninghame* [1906] 2 Ch 34). However, although the directors have control over the company's management, they are still subject to its constitution. Thus the members always retain their rights:

(a) to change the powers given to the directors in the articles (section 9); and

(b) to dismiss a director by ordinary resolution (section 303).

These rights are protected by statute and cannot be taken away by the articles. However, voting rights can be dictated by the articles in such a way as to give additional votes to certain shares in certain circumstances (see paragraph 1.42, above).

The power given to directors is also circumscribed by the common law duties which prevent them abusing their position. These are discussed in Chapter 3, but can be summarised as a duty to show good faith and to display appropriate skill and care.

2.13 Specific powers in the articles

The articles often set out a number of specific powers for the directors. The main powers specifically given to directors in the 1985 version of Table A enable them to carry out the following acts:

(a) Manage the business of the company (article 70).

(b) Call general meetings of the company (article 37).

(c) Appoint an agent to act on the company's behalf (article 71).

(d) Delegate their powers to a committee or managing director (article 72).

(e) Appoint an additional director to fill a casual vacancy (article 79).

(f) Appoint a managing director or appoint a director to any executive position (article 84).

(g) Pay gratuities and pensions to former directors or members of their family (article 87).

(h) Regulate their proceedings as they think fit (article 88).

(i) Appoint or remove the chairman (article 91).

(j) Appoint or remove the secretary (article 99).

(k) Authorise use of the company's seal (article 101).

(l) Pay interim dividends (article 103).

(m) Capitalise profits if authorised by the members (article 110).

(n) Exercise various powers in relation to calls on and transfers of shares (articles 12–28, see paragraph 6.21, below).

Individual directors also have certain rights and powers under Table A:

(a) The chairman presides at general meetings (article 42).

(b) Any director has the right to speak at any general meeting even if he is not himself a member (article 44).

(c) A director may appoint an alternate (article 65).

2.14 Delegation of powers by directors

In principle, directors must exercise their power collectively through the authority of the board (*Re Haycraft Gold Reduction and Mining Co* [1900] 2 Ch 230). In practice, the articles usually allow the board to appoint a managing director and to delegate any of their powers to any of their number. The 1985 version of Table A makes the following provisions:

(a) The directors may appoint one or more of their number to the office of managing director or to any other executive office (article 84).

(b) The board may delegate its powers on any basis it chooses to any committee consisting of one or more of its members (article 72). *Re Fireproof Doors Ltd, Umney v Fireproof Doors Ltd* [1916] 2 Ch 142 had already established that a committee may consist of one person.

2.20 POWER TO BIND THE COMPANY IN CONTRACTS

While most people dealing with a company director assume without question that he can enter into a valid contract on the company's behalf, they are in fact acting on three implicit assumptions:

(a) that the company itself has the power to enter into the transaction;

(b) that the board of directors is entitled to exercise this power; and

(c) that the individual director has been delegated with sufficient authority to act on the company's behalf.

Where a director acts within his delegated authority, the company is bound by the acts of the director under the normal rules of agent and principal. If the director has not been given executive power by the board or the articles he has, in principle, no power to bind the company. However, even when the director exceeds his or the company's powers, the law usually allows third parties to enforce the contract against the company. These considerations are discussed in the following paragraphs.

2.21 Transactions outside the company's capacity or the power of the board of directors

The threat of transaction outside of the objects clause of a company being *ultra vires* and void has been almost removed following revisions made to the Companies Act 1985 by the Companies Act 1989. Section 35 provides that 'the validity of an act done by a company shall not be called into question on the ground of lack of capacity by reason of anything in the company's memorandum'. This does not prevent a member of the company bringing a restraining action in respect of an act beyond the company's capacity, unless that act is to be done to fulfil a legal obligation arising from a previous act of the company. An *ultra vires* act may be ratified by special resolution (see paragraph 2.24, below).

A person dealing with a company in good faith may assume that the power of the board of directors to bind the company, or to authorise others to do so, is free of any limitation under the company's constitution. A third party is therefore protected when the directors, while acting within the powers of the company, exceed the authority vested in them by the constitution. This does not prevent a member of the company bringing a restraining action in respect of an act beyond the power of the directors, unless that act is to be done to fulfil a legal obligation arising from a previous act of the company (section 35A). Nor does it affect the liability of the directors, or any other person, for the act.

A person shall not be regarded as acting in bad faith only because he knows that an act is beyond the powers of the directors under the company's constitution. A person is also presumed to have acted in good faith unless the contrary is proved (section 35A).

For these purposes limitations on the directors under the company's constitution include those arising from a resolution or agreement of the members or a class of shareholders (section 35A).

The reliefs discussed above do not affect the provisions concerning *ultra vires* transactions with directors of the company or persons connected with them (section 322A, see paragraph 2.22, below). Also the reliefs only apply to companies that are charities in certain circumstances (Charities Act 1960 section 30B(1) and Companies Act 1989 section 112(3)).

A party to a transaction with a company is not bound to enquire as to the power of the company or the directors to enter into it (section 35B).

2.22 Transactions involving directors

Special provisions apply to transactions between a company and a director of that company or of its holding company, or a person connected with the director (section 322A).

If the board of directors exceed their powers in respect of such a transaction it is voidable by the company except in the following circumstances.

(a) Restitution of any money or other asset that was the subject of the transaction is not possible.

(b) The company is indemnified for loss or damage arising from the transaction.

(c) If it would affect rights acquired *bona fide* for value and without notice of the directors' breach of power by a person who was not party to the transaction.

(d) The transaction is ratified by the company in general meeting.

Any director of the company who authorised the transaction and any director or connected person party to the transaction can be required to account for any gain they have made or to indemnify the company for any loss or damage (section 322A). However a person other than a director of the company is not so liable if he can show that he did not know the directors were exceeding their powers at the time of the transaction.

2.23 Apparent authority

A director can bind the company in a transaction which would normally be within the power of a director of his type, even if his powers have been restricted by the articles or the board. Thus a third party can assume that a properly appointed managing director has been delegated all the normal powers (*Kreditbank Cassel GmbH v Schenkers* [1927] 1 KB 826).

A director 'held out' by the company as being the managing director can bind the company even if he has not been formally appointed. In *Freeman and Lockyer v Buckhurst Park Properties (Mangal) Ltd* [1964] 2 QB 480 the articles contained a power to appoint a managing director, although no appointment was made. The board allowed one of the directors to undertake the management of the company, in the course of which he engaged a firm of architects. The company subsequently refused to pay the architect's bill, on the ground that the individual director had exceeded his authority. The Court of Appeal held that the company was bound by the contract since the articles allowed for the company to appoint a managing director and it was reasonable for an outsider to assume that a director who appeared to be the managing director could enter into a contract on the company's behalf. To take advantage of this case it is necessary for the outsider to have relied on representations by those with actual authority (in this case the other directors) to the effect that the individual director had the appropriate authority.

2.24 Ratification of transactions

A transaction within the powers of the company can be ratified by the members in general meeting (*Bamford v Bamford* [1970] Ch 212). (If a director merely exceeds his individual authority his action can of course be ratified by the board.)

A transaction outside the capacity of a company may be ratified by special resolution. Such a resolution does not affect any liability incurred by the directors, which must be agreed to by a separate special resolution (section 35). Such ratification does not affect the provisions in respect of transactions with directors (section 322A, see paragraph 2.22, above) and is only possible for charitable companies in certain circumstances (Charities Act 1960 section 30B(1) and Companies Act 1989 section 112(3)).

2.25 Defects in appointment

Section 285 states that the acts of a director (or manager) are valid notwithstanding any defect that may afterwards be discovered in his appointment or qualification.

The provisions of this section have been narrowly interpreted in the past. Thus in *Morris v Kanssen* [1946] AC 459 it was held that the provision could only cure a defective appointment and did not operate where there was no appointment at all or where the appointment was made by persons with no power to do so. The section covers only some slip or irregularity where there was an intention to make an appointment by persons with the appropriate power.

2.30 PERSONAL LIABILITY OF DIRECTORS FOR CONTRACTS

Although the director when acting as agent binds the company and not himself, there are certain circumstances in which he becomes personally liable.

(a) *Pre-incorporation contracts* If a promoter attempts to contract on behalf of the company before it has been formed then, subject to any agreement to the contrary, he is personally liable (section 36).

(b) *Non-disclosure of company's interest* The ordinary rules of an agent contracting on behalf of an undisclosed principal would make a director personally liable if he failed to disclose the company's interest.

(c) *Cheques* A director who signs a company cheque is personally liable on it unless he makes it clear that he signs as a representative of the company (Bills of Exchange Act 1882, section 26). Modern practice is to print the company's full name on cheques, in which case a director is not personally liable when he signs his own name (*Bondina Ltd v Rollaway Shower Blinds Ltd* [1986] 1 All ER 564). If a director signs a cheque (or a bill of exchange or an order of goods) in such a way as to make it clear that he is not personally liable on it he will still incur personal liability if the company's name does not appear in full on the cheque etc (section 349). The full and correct name must be used; the only permissible abbreviations are Ltd or plc (or their Welsh equivalents).

(d) *Breach of warranty of authority* If a director contracts on behalf of a company when he has no authority to do so he is not personally liable, but may be liable in damages for breach of implied warranty of authority.

2.40 TORTS AND CRIMES

A tort is a breach of a legal duty that gives rise to a civil action for damages. A crime is an offence against the Crown that is punishable by a fine or imprisonment or both. Normally, an officer, agent or servant of a company who commits a tort or crime is personally liable for his action. He may well also be in breach of duty to the company.

The company itself, as a legal person, can be the victim of a tort or crime, but can clearly only commit such an offence through the agency of a living person. The circumstances in which the company can be made responsible for the actions of its living agents are dealt with in the following paragraphs.

2.41 Torts committed by companies

Torts include, for example, negligence, trespass and libel, but exclude breaches of contract (for which separate remedies are available). A company, like any other principal or employer, is liable for torts committed by its agents or employees *in the course of its business*. Directors are not personally liable for the company's torts unless directly involved in the wrongdoing – in which case they may be jointly liable with the company.

2.42 Company crimes

The position with regard to crimes is more complicated. Certain crimes, such as rape or bigamy, are clearly beyond the capacity of an artificial person and cannot be committed by a company. Furthermore, whereas a civil case is decided on the balance of probabilities, in a criminal case it is necessary to prove guilt beyond a reasonable doubt. As a result for most serious crimes it is necessary to show *mens rea* (guilty intention). A company has no mind and cannot, therefore, have a guilty intention (although the intentions of certain individuals may be ascribed to it in certain circumstances). However, there are a number of offences, particularly under modern statutes, for which guilty intention does not have to be proved. These are known as offences of strict liability. The distinction between the two types of offence is important in that whereas a company cannot normally be guilty of a crime for which guilty intention must be proved, it can be guilty of an offence of strict liability.

2.43 Crimes involving guilty intention

In cases where guilty intention must be proved, the living persons responsible for the crime are personally liable but, as a general rule, their criminal intentions cannot be ascribed to the company. However, in *Lennard's Carrying Co Ltd v Asiatic Petroleum Co Ltd* [1915] AC 705 it was established that the mental state of persons *controlling* the company could be attributed to the company itself. In this way the acts of the directors can become the acts of the company for the purpose of establishing guilty intention, so that a company can be convicted of offences involving criminal volition, such as dishonesty.

Successive cases have left some doubts about which officers, agents or servants of a company can represent its directing mind and will do so in the commission of a crime and so impose vicarious liability upon it. The latest authority is *Tesco Supermarkets Ltd v Nattrass* [1972] AC 153 in which the House of Lords established that 'the acts or omissions of shop managers were not the acts of the company itself'. However, if a board were to delegate part of its functions it is possible that the manager could become, within the area of his authority, the embodiment of the company for the purpose of criminal liability. The judgment unfortunately appears to have been reached on the basis of a stratified management under which the board delegated certain operational functions within a chain of command, but remained in control. In other cases the management structure may not be so clear. Nevertheless it is established that the acts of employees in subordinate positions can never be the acts of the company (unless otherwise provided by the statute).

2.44 Offences of strict liability

Strict liability arises where breaking the law is in itself an offence, irrespective of guilty intention. There are examples in the Companies Act (for example, a failure to maintain a register of directors) as well as under other statutes. In such instances an offence by the company is not generally an offence by the directors unless specified as such in the statute. However, in most cases the relevant Act does indeed specify that the directors are personally liable. (*Directors' Personal Liabilities*, published by the Institute of Directors, documents the numerous statutory provisions under which directors may become vicariously liable for corporate offences.)

2.45 Personal liability for offences under the Companies Act

The Companies Act itself is particularly rich in offences. Schedule 24 lists 150 of them with their penalties, which range from a fine up to seven years' imprisonment (for fraud and similar offences). Various formulae for creating personal liability are used in the Act. In many cases the company's officers are made personally liable if they are 'in default'. An officer is in default if he 'knowingly and wilfully authorises or permits the default, refusal or contravention mentioned in the enactment' (section 730). In effect this formula restores the requirement for a director (although not the company) to have a guilty intention before he can be convicted of the offence. For example, a non-executive director would be protected unless he was directly involved in the offence or deliberately ignored the consequences of the company's action.

Some requirements under the Act are the responsibility not of the company but of the directors. This occurs, for example, in relation to the requirement to file accounts (section 242). In these cases an individual director is usually liable unless he takes 'all reasonable steps' to ensure compliance. All reasonable steps would probably be satisfied by delegation to an appropriate official (see paragraph 3.33, below).

2.46 Criminal liability for fraud

A director or other officer who publishes a misleading, false or deceptive statement with the intention of deceiving members or creditors is guilty of a criminal offence and liable for up to seven years' imprisonment (Theft Act 1968, section 19). The offence is committed if the document when taken as a whole is deceptive, even if it contains no specific falsehoods (*R v Lord Kylsant* [1932] 1 KB 442).

Sections 15 and 16 of the Theft Act 1968 deal with obtaining property or 'pecuniary advantage' by deception. A director or other officer who consents to or connives at the commission of such an offence is himself liable (Theft Act 1968, section 18). These provisions of the Theft Act 1968 do not apply in Scotland.

3 Common law duties of directors

The law does not impose an all-embracing code of conduct on directors. Some duties, certainly, are laid down by statute, but many are found only in common law. As a result, specific duties tend to be discovered only when they have been breached and the courts are attempting to effect a remedy.

However, it has been established that a director owes two types of duty to the company, a 'fiduciary' duty and a duty of skill and care.

The fiduciary duty requires a director to act honestly in his dealings with or on behalf of the company. This means that as a board, the directors must act in good faith in the best interests of the company, and exercise their powers for a proper purpose. An individual director should not allow his personal interests to conflict with the interests of the company, nor derive any personal profit from his position beyond that which the company pays him.

The duty of skill and care has been held to have three essentials:

- *a director is not an expert and should not be presumed, merely by virtue of his office, to have skills he does not in fact possess;*
- *a director need only display, in relation to his duties, the reasonable care of an ordinary man;*
- *a director is entitled, in the absence of suspicious circumstances, to delegate.*

These rules were actually formulated in 1925, and need to be viewed cautiously in the light of modern standards. In particular, executive directors are normally employed for their expertise, and a director accepting an executive function is presumed to have the skills necessary to perform it. Any director, whether executive or non-executive, would be expected to apply any relevant qualifications or experience he might have when carrying out his duties. Nevertheless, a director is not likely to be held liable merely for making an error of judgement.

If a director breaches any of his common law duties, the company can sue to recover its property or for damages as compensation for any loss. The company is also entitled to any personal profit the director may have made by exploiting his position. If the company cannot or will not sue (for example, where the wrongdoer controls it), one or more shareholders may be able to bring an action on behalf of the company.

In some cases the directors' actions can be ratified by ordinary resolution of the members in general meeting. What is ratifiable is not clearly established, although, for example, secret profits and failures of skill and care have been ratified in certain cases.

3.10 TYPES OF DUTY

As we have seen, the company director can be to some extent regarded as a trustee and as an agent. The conventional analysis of directors' duties also follows these two analogies by ascribing to directors two types of duty.

(a) *Fiduciary duty* This is the duty of good faith owed by a trustee who must not abuse his position of trust by, for example, making a personal profit.

(b) *Duty of skill and care* As an agent the director is not only under a fiduciary duty to the company, but also under a duty to exercise skill and care when acting on the company's behalf.

Of course, a director may also have more specific duties to the company as laid down, for example, in a contract of employment or where he is acting as a professional adviser.

3.11 Duties to whom?

Directors' duties are owed to the company, not to the individual members. In *Percival v Wright* [1902] 2 Ch 421 the directors purchased shares from the plaintiffs while secretly negotiating to sell the company at a more favourable price. The court declined to upset the contract remarking that premature disclosure of the negotiations 'might well be against the best interests of the company'. (The implications of insider dealing are discussed in paragraph 4.40 ff, below.)

However, the directors may in particular circumstances owe duties to individual shareholders: for example, when they undertake to act as the shareholders' agents (*Allen v Hyatt* (1914) 30 TLR 444).

Directors have a duty to take into account the interests of employees as well as the interests of members (section 309). The statutory duty is owed to and enforceable by the company, not by the employees directly, so acts benefiting employees must also further the interests of the company. This provision does not change the directors' duties in a going concern, since benefits for the workforce had been held to be in the interests of the company (*Hutton v West Cork Rly Co* (1883) 23 Ch D 654).

However, if the company closes or transfers the whole or part of its business it has the power to make provision for employees and former employees even if it is not in its best interests to do so (section 719). This power is normally exercisable by ordinary resolution, unless the memorandum or articles specify a directors' resolution or require a greater majority of members. This section reverses the case of *Parke v Daily News Ltd* [1962] Ch 927 in which it was held that a company could not make *ex gratia* payments to employees on the sale of a major part of its business.

Directors have not been held to have a general duty to creditors. *Brady v Brady* (1987) 3 BCC 535 and *Liquidator of West Mercia Safetyware Ltd v Dodd* (1988) 4 BCC 30 suggest that a duty of care to creditors arises if a company is insolvent. In *Winkworth v Edward Baron Development Co Ltd* [1987] 1 All ER 114, it was said that property should not be dissipated or exploited for the benefit of the directors themselves to the prejudice of the creditors. There are a number of circumstances in which directors can incur personal liability for the company's debts. Most of these apply only in the event of the company's winding up and are dealt with in Chapter 11. In particular, under the wrongful trading provisions of the Insolvency Act 1986, a director has a duty to take every step that he ought to have taken to minimise the potential loss to creditors from the time at which he knew or ought to have known that the company had no reasonable prospect of avoiding insolvent liquidation (see paragraph 11.23, below). Directors can also be made directly liable to individual creditors if they act while disqualified (see paragraph 1.35, above) or if they breach the rules on re-using the names of insolvent companies (see paragraph 11.24, below).

3.20 FIDUCIARY DUTY

An individual director must act in good faith in his dealings with or on behalf of the company and exercise the powers and fulfil the duties of his office honestly.

3.21 Duty to act in good faith

Directors acting as a board have a duty to act in good faith in what they consider to be the best interests of the company. This duty is a subjective one: 'Directors must exercise their discretion *bona fide* in what they consider – not what a court may consider – is in the interests of the company, and not for any collateral purpose' (*Re Smith & Fawcett Ltd* [1942] 1 All ER 542). The courts allow the directors absolute discretion, interfering only if no reasonable director could have believed that a course of action was in the best interests of the company.

However, a director acting honestly but not in the best interests of the company is in breach of duty. Thus in *Re W & M Roith Ltd* [1967] 1 All ER 427 a director in poor health who entered into a service contract providing for a generous widow's pension in the event of his death was held not to be acting *bona fide* in the interests of the company, which was not held to the contract.

3.22 Duty to exercise powers for a proper purpose

In general, the directors are not allowed to exercise their powers in such a way as to prevent the majority of the members exercising their constitutional rights. Much of the case law involving misuse of powers involves directors issuing shares for a purpose other than to raise capital needed by the company. Insofar as they relate specifically to the issue of shares, the common law rules obliging directors to act for a proper purpose have been augmented by statutory provisions (see paragraph 6.21, below). However, the following cases also illustrate the wider principle involved.

In *Punt v Symons & Co Ltd* [1903] 2 Ch 506 the directors issued shares to five additional members in order to obtain approval of a special resolution securing their own position. The court ruled that this was not a *bona fide* exercise of their power for the advantage of the company as a whole.

Even if the directors are acting in good faith in the interests of the company as a whole, they must still use their powers for the purposes for which they were intended. If they use these powers for another purpose there is a breach of duty. In *Hogg v Cramphorn Ltd* [1967] Ch 254 the directors issued shares with special voting rights to the trustees of a scheme set up for the benefit of the company's employees, in order to forestall a take-over. It was held that although the directors had acted in good faith they had breached their duty to the company by making improper use of their power to issue shares.

However, it was also held that the directors' breach of duty could be ratified by the company in general meeting (with the newly issued shares not voting). This decision was approved by the Court of Appeal in *Bamford v Bamford* [1970] Ch 212. In this case the directors issued 500,000 shares to a third party, also to defend a take-over bid. This breach of duty was held to be ratifiable.

The directors' powers to issue shares are normally defined in the articles (Table A does not confer a general power). Section 80 prevents directors from issuing shares unless authorised by the company in general meeting or by the articles. Cases turning on what is the proper purpose for an issue of shares can thus depend on the construction of the articles.

In *Howard Smith Ltd v Ampol Petroleum Ltd* [1974] AC 821 directors who issued shares in order to secure a majority in favour of a take-over were held to have acted for an improper purpose, although the court concluded that it is 'too narrow an approach to say that the only valid purpose for which shares may be issued is to raise capital for the company'. This was a Privy Council decision and as such is persuasive but not binding on other courts.

Where directors act for mixed purposes, various Commonwealth cases have decided that it is the primary purpose which must be judged proper or improper. A reference in the *Howard Smith* case to the 'substantial purpose for which it was exercised' suggests a similar approach.

3.23 Conflicts of interest

A director must not put himself in a position where there is an actual or potential conflict between his personal interest and his duty to the company. The effect of this at common law is that a director may not enter into a valid contract (other than a service contract) with the company, even indirectly, unless the company gives its approval in general meeting, or the articles allow it.

In *Aberdeen Rly Co v Blaikie Bros* (1854) 2 Eq Rep 1281 the railway company agreed to buy iron chairs from a partnership of which its chairman was managing partner. The House of Lords held that the company was entitled to avoid the contract irrespective of its merits:

> 'it is a rule of universal application that no-one having such [fiduciary] duties to discharge shall be allowed to enter into engagements in which he has or can have a personal interest conflicting, or which possibly may conflict, with the interests of those whom he is bound to protect'.

The strict application of this principle would often work to the detriment of companies, and it is established that disclosure by the director of his interest may validate the contract. In *North-West Transportation Co Ltd v Beatty* (1887) 12 App Cas 589 it was established that a contract voidable because of a director's interest is ratifiable by the company in general meeting, and that the director may vote as a shareholder on the resolution.

Disclosure by the director of his interest to a quorum of directors is probably insufficient to validate the contract under the law as it stands (although there is no modern authority). In practice, however, most modern articles render such contracts enforceable subject to disclosure to the board. Article 85 of Table A specifically permits a director to have an interest in a contract 'subject to the provisions of the Act and provided that he had disclosed to the directors the nature and extent of any material interest'.

Section 317 imposes a requirement, which cannot be waived by the articles, for a director to disclose to the board any interest he may have in a contract with the company (see paragraph 10.52, below). If the interest is material it must also be disclosed in the annual accounts (see paragraph 10.52, below). Such disclosure must be made to the full board, not a sub-committee (*Guinness plc v Saunders* [1990] 2 AC 663).

By extension, a director must not 'fetter his discretion' to act in the best interests of the company by, for example, a contract with an outsider. But he is not under an obligation to refrain from competing with his company or even from becoming a director in a rival company (*Bell v Lever Bros Ltd* [1932] AC 161). According to Lord Denning, though, in *Scottish Co-op Wholesale Society Ltd v Meyer* [1959] AC 324, he risks an application under section 459 (protection of company's members against unfair prejudice) if he subordinates the interests of the one company to those of the other.

Statutory requirements in respect of substantial property transactions are dealt with in paragraph 4.20, below.

3.24 Secret profits

A director's fiduciary position precludes him from taking a personal profit from any opportunities that result from his directorship, even if he is acting honestly and for the good of the company. Any profit arising in such circumstances must be accounted for to the company – that is, paid over to the company. This applies whether the profit arises from a contract with the company or a third party.

Even if the director's profit would not have accrued to the company, he must still account for it if the opportunity to make it arose through his directorship. In *Regal (Hastings) Ltd v Gulliver* [1942] 1 All ER 378, Regal owned one cinema and wished to acquire two others in order to sell all three as a going concern. The directors formed a subsidiary to acquire the two cinemas, but because Regal had insufficient capital to make the purchase the directors themselves took up some shares in the subsidiary. The shares in Regal and its subsidiary were eventually sold at a profit. The House of Lords held that Regal (now controlled by a new board) was entitled to recover the personal profit made by the former directors, because the opportunity to make the profit arose only through knowledge they had gained as directors.

Although it is not a defence that the directors acted honestly and in good faith, the company in general meeting can often ratify the directors' actions and allow them to keep the profit. In *Regal* the directors had the necessary majority, and it was stated that they would have been protected by resolution of the shareholders (but because they were acting in good faith did not realise approval was necessary). However, in *Cook v Deeks* [1916] 1 AC 554 directors who acquired a contract they had a duty to acquire for the company were not allowed to ratify their action by resolution in general meeting. The point of law distinguishing the cases is not clear, but it may be that whereas in *Regal* the opportunity to make the profit could not be taken by the company, in *Cook v Deeks* the company was deprived of just such an opportunity. It is likely, therefore, that directors would be precluded from voting their majority shareholdings if they have committed fraud on the minority by misappropriating company assets.

In *Aveling Barford Ltd v Perion Ltd* (1989) 5 BCC 677 the disposal of a property at an undervalue was held to be a breach of fiduciary duty and Perion, the purchaser, a constructive trustee. Aveling Barford was wholly owned by an individual who also controlled Perion. The transaction was held to be incapable of being approved or ratified by the shareholder as it was in effect an unauthorised return of capital, Aveling Barford having no distributable reserves at the time.

A director cannot escape his duty to account for a personal profit by resigning before he takes it (*Industrial Development Consultants Ltd v Cooley* [1972] 2 All ER 162). However, in the Canadian case *Peso Silver Mines Ltd v Cropper* (1966) 58 DLR (2d) 1 it was held that a director is free to make an investment on his own account after his company has considered the proposition and *bona fide* decided against it.

3.30 DUTY OF SKILL AND CARE

The directors' fiduciary duties impose on them a largely negative obligation to do nothing which conflicts with the company's interests. But when they *are* acting in the company's interests they are also expected to exercise whatever skill they possess and reasonable care.

The leading case on the nature and extent of the duty of skill and care is *Re City Equitable Fire Insurance Co Ltd* [1925] Ch 407, in which three basic principles were formulated:

(a) A director is not an expert, and need only display skills he actually possesses.

(b) A director need not devote his continuous attention to the business.

(c) A director is entitled, in the absence of suspicious circumstances, to rely on others.

City Equitable is still the leading authority, but its principles are very much founded on the idea of the Victorian gentleman director. The extent to which its principles still hold good is discussed in the following paragraphs.

3.31 Degree of skill

A director is not expected to exercise a level of skill he does not have.

> 'A director need not exhibit in the performance of his duties a greater degree of skill than may reasonably be expected from a person of his knowledge and experience. A director of a life assurance company, for instance, does not guarantee that he has the skill of an actuary or of a physician.'

(*Re City Equitable Fire Insurance Co Ltd* [1925] Ch 407.)

The level of skill required of a director is therefore subjective, in that he is not expected, merely by virtue of his office, to possess any particular skills: his performance must be judged by the way he applies any skills which he actually has. However, an objective level of skill may be imposed in two circumstances:

(a) An executive director with a contract of service would probably be required to display an objective level of skill implied in the contract. (There is no specific authority for this in the case of directors, but skilled employees have been held to owe such a duty.)

(b) In the case of an insolvent company, a director faces personal liability for wrongful trading if he does not display both the general knowledge, skill and experience that he actually has and also that which might reasonably be expected of someone carrying out his function within the company (this is more fully discussed in paragraph 11.23, below).

In *Dorchester Finance Co Ltd v Stebbing* (1977) [1989] BCLC 498 it was held that two non-executive directors, both experienced accountants, had been negligent in their duties as directors in signing blank cheques at the request of the one full-time director. In considering a director's duties and the level of skill and care required it was held that no distinction was to be drawn between executive and non-executive directors, the test being dependent upon the directors' knowledge and experience.

3.32 Attention to the business

A director must attend diligently to the affairs of the company. In performing his duties he must display the 'reasonable care ... an ordinary man might be expected to take in the same circumstances on his own behalf' (*Re Brazilian Rubber Plantations and Estates Ltd* [1911] 1 Ch 425). Mere errors of judgement have been held not to breach the duty of skill and care (*Lagunas Nitrate Co v Lagunas Syndicate* [1899] 2 Ch 392).

It was held in *City Equitable* that 'a director is not bound to give continuous attention to the affairs of the company. His duties are of an intermittent nature'. This dictum is clearly more appropriate to the circumstances of a non-executive director, and refers specifically to attendance at board meetings (dealt with in paragraph 8.10, below). An executive director's service contract normally requires that he devotes his full attention to the business of the company.

3.33 Reliance on others

A director is entitled to rely on his fellow directors and officers of the company. Thus in *Dovey v Cory* [1901] AC 477 it was held that a director was entitled to rely on a subordinate 'put in a position of trust for the express purpose of attending to the detail of management'.

Similarly in *City Equitable* it was said, 'in respect of duties ... that may properly be left to some other official, a director is, in the absence of grounds for suspicion, justified in trusting that official to perform such duties honestly'. Thus in this case the directors were entitled to sign cheques which appeared to be properly authorised although subsequently put to an unauthorised use.

The absence of suspicious circumstances was also relied on in *Huckerby v Elliott* [1970] 1 All ER 189 in which a director failed to enquire whether a gaming licence had been obtained but had no grounds for suspicion.

Directors may also rely on the opinions of an outside expert, and, in fact may be negligent if they do not obtain such an opinion in appropriate circumstances. (For example, *Fry v Tapson* (1884) 28 Ch D 268, *Re Duomatic Ltd* [1969] 2 Ch 365.)

However, directors cannot absolve themselves entirely of responsibility by delegation to others. For example, in *Selangor United Rubber Estates Ltd v Cradock* [1967] 2 All ER 1255 directors were held liable where they should have been aware of a wrong, even though they were in fact ignorant of it. The Department of Trade Inspectors in their report on *First Re-investment Trust Ltd* [1974] also rejected the *City Equitable* principle in a case where, they said, the director should have exercised his own judgement in a company dominated by one man. (See also disagreement among directors, paragraph 8.20, below.)

3.40 BREACH OF DUTY

3.41 Liability for breach of duty

A director who fails in his duty to the company has unlimited liability for any resultant loss, even if he has not himself made a personal gain (as, for example, in the case of negligence). Any attempt by the company to exempt a director from liability for negligence, default, breach of duty or breach of trust is void (section 310). However, the company can purchase and maintain insurance against such a liability or indemnify the director against the costs of a successful defence of a criminal or civil action. The court also has power to exempt a director from liability if he has acted honestly and reasonably and having regard to all the circumstances ought fairly to be excused (section 727). This defence is not available in respect of wrongful trading (*Halls v David* (1989) 5 BCC 399). Directors can also take advantage of professional liability insurance to indemnify themselves against liability to the company and third parties.

3.42 Remedies for breach of duty

Assuming the company does not want to ratify a director's breach of duty (see paragraph 3.43, below) it has six legal remedies:

(a) An injunction to prevent a director from carrying out a breach of duty in the future or from continuing in a breach of duty.

(b) Damages as compensation for loss occasioned by a director's breach of duty (for example, negligence).

(c) Restoration of company property, provided the property is traceable and has not been acquired for value by an innocent third party.

(d) An account of profits made by the director (see paragraph 3.24, above).

(e) Rescission of a contract in which a director has an undisclosed interest.

(f) Dismissal of the director (see paragraph 1.42, above).

3.43 Ratification of breaches of duty

It is generally open to the company to ratify a director's breach of duty and several circumstances in which it can do so have already been discussed in previous paragraphs:

(a) On allotment of shares for an improper purpose (paragraph 3.22, above).

(b) A failure to disclose an interest in a contract (paragraph 3.23, above).

(c) The obtaining of a secret profit not available to the company (paragraph 3.24, above).

(d) A failure of skill and care, if not fraudulent (*Pavlides v Jensen* [1956] Ch 565).

(e) An act which is *ultra vires* the company (paragraph 2.24, above).

However, certain breaches cannot be ratified by the company:

(a) Infringement of the individual rights of shareholders, such as an improper refusal to register a share transfer (*Re Smith & Fawcett Ltd* [1942] Ch 304).

(b) A breach which is fraudulent or dishonest (*Mason v Harris* (1879) 11 Ch D 97).

(c) In the circumstances of *Cook v Deeks* (see paragraph 3.24, above) the company was not allowed to ratify a secret profit taken at the expense of the company.

(d) In certain circumstances, an act which is *ultra vires* a charitable company (see paragraph 2.24, above).

4 Statutory duties of directors

The general principles governing directors' conduct discussed in the previous chapter are augmented by a range of specific duties imposed by statute. Some of these duties are actually imposed on the company itself but devolve upon the directors as part of their general management responsibilities: for example, the requirement to keep proper accounting records and to file an annual return. Other duties are imposed on directors themselves, generally taking the form either of a restriction of a particular activity or a requirement to disclose it, or both.

Many of the relevant provisions of the Act are drawn together under the heading 'Enforcement of fair dealing by directors', and derive from attempts to curb particular abuses that have arisen in practice. Many of these provisions fall conveniently into the subject matter of other chapters. Those that do not are dealt with in this chapter.

There are a number of statutory restrictions on directors taking financial advantage of their position. They are not allowed to receive tax-free remuneration and members must approve any compensation for loss of office. Directors' service contracts cannot exceed five years without members' approval, and must be made available for inspection.

Requiring directors to disclose details about themselves and their dealings with the company is a common technique adopted in the Act to discourage directors from abusing their powers and to reassure shareholders that no such abuse has occurred.

Directors must disclose their interests in the shares and debentures of the company and other group companies. A register of these interests must be maintained and made available for inspection by the public. It is a criminal offence for directors of listed companies to deal in options in the company's shares, or to deal in the shares on the basis of inside knowledge. It is also an offence to pass on inside information to someone likely to use it for the purpose of dealing, and for anyone receiving such information to use it for dealing.

The company must maintain a register of directors and secretaries, which must be available for inspection. Directors' names can only appear on company correspondence if the names of all the directors are shown.

Some disclosures – such as interests in contracts with the company – are initially made to the board, which decides on further disclosure (although see also Chapter 10 which deals with loans to directors and other transactions). Certain other information, such as details of directors' service contracts, is in theory available only to members; but most is filed with the registrar and therefore publicly available.

Various other documents must be made available by the company for inspection by the public:

- *register of members;*
- *register of debenture holders (if a register is kept);*
- *minutes of general meetings (minutes must be kept of directors' meetings, but they need not be made public);*
- *register of charges;*
- *register of substantial interests in shares.*

The company must also file an annual return with the registrar setting out much of this information.

Finally, there are a number of circumstances in which the Department of Trade and Industry can initiate an investigation into the company's affairs. Directors – along with other officers and agents of the company – are required to co-operate with the investigating officials.

4.10 ENFORCEMENT OF FAIR DEALING

Part X of the Companies Act 1985 (sections 311 to 347) draws together many of the provisions introduced by previous Acts for the enforcement of fair dealing by directors. The Act groups the provisions under three sub-headings:

(a) Restrictions on directors taking financial advantage.

(b) Share dealings by directors and their families (see paragraphs 4.31 and 4.32, below).

(c) Restrictions on a company's power to make loans etc to directors and persons connected with them (see Chapter 10).

The restrictions on directors taking financial advantage are as follows:

(a) Section 311 prohibits tax-free payments to directors (see Chapter 9).

(b) Section 312 requires members' approval for certain payments to directors for loss of office (see Chapter 9).

(c) Section 313 requires members' approval for any payment to a director for loss of office in connection with the transfer of the whole or part of the company's business (see paragraph 6.51, below).

(d) Section 314 requires a director who receives a payment in connection with a take-over of the company to ensure that details of the payment are circulated to shareholders with the offer document (see paragraph 6.51, below).

(e) Section 317 requires a director to disclose to the board any interest he has in any contract with the company (see paragraph 10.52, below).

(f) Section 318 requires directors' service contracts to be available for inspection (see paragraph 4.53, below).

(g) Section 319 provides that a director's service contract must not exceed five years unless members approve (see paragraph 9.20, below).

(h) Section 320 prohibits substantial property transactions with a director except in certain circumstances (see paragraph 4.20, below).

4.20 SUBSTANTIAL PROPERTY TRANSACTIONS INVOLVING DIRECTORS

A director of a company or of its holding company may not enter into an arrangement to acquire from or transfer to the company a non-cash asset unless one of the following applies:

(a) the arrangement is approved in advance by members in general meeting and, if a director of the holding company, by a resolution in general meeting of the holding company (section 320);

(b) the arrangement is affirmed by members of the company and holding company, if applicable, within a reasonable period (section 322);

(c) the value of the non-cash asset is less than £2,000; or, if greater, the lower of £100,000 or 10% of the company's net assets (section 320);

(d) the arrangement is between a wholly-owned subsidiary and either its holding company or a fellow wholly-owned subsidiary (section 321);

(e) the arrangement is with a company which is being wound up (except a member's voluntary winding up) (section 321);

(f) the director is acquiring a non-cash asset in his capacity as a member (for example, a rights issue) (section 321).

An 'arrangement' is deliberately undefined so as not to restrict it to, for example, a legally enforceable contract. A 'non-cash asset' means any property or interest in property other than cash (which includes foreign currency), and includes the creation of an interest in property (such as a lease) or the discharge of any liability (section 739).

The arrangement is voidable by the company unless (section 322):

(a) restitution of any cash or property involved in the arrangement is no longer possible; or

(b) the company has been indemnified for its loss; or

(c) rights acquired *bona fide* and without notice of the contravention by a third party would be affected.

It was considered *per curiam* in *Niltan Carson Ltd v Hawthorne* (1987) 3 BCC 454 that a contract entered into contrary to what is now section 320 was not illegal *ab initio*. It remained valid and binding until avoided at the instance of the company.

The restriction on substantial property transactions extends to shadow directors and persons connected with directors (see paragraph 10.11, below).

4.30 SHARE DEALINGS

4.31 Disclosure of interests in shares and debentures

Each director is obliged, within five days of his appointment, to notify the company in writing of his interests in shares and debentures of the company and group companies (section 324). Any subsequent change in the interests must be notified within five days of the 'event' which causes the change. An event is something such as a sale, purchase, gift or inheritance.

A director for this purpose includes a shadow director and an alternate director from the moment he is appointed to the time he is relieved of his post and not just when he is performing the duties of a director.

The interests of a director's spouse and infant children, unless they are also directors, are treated as the interests of the director (section 328 and Schedule 7, paragraph 2B).

The term 'interest' is defined very widely in Schedule 13:

(a) an interest in shares or debentures includes any interest of any kind whatsoever;

(b) any restraints or restrictions on the exercise of any rights attached to the interest are disregarded;

(c) it is immaterial that the shares or debentures in which a person has an interest are unidentifiable.

Specific rules for determining which interests are to be included in and excluded from the disclosure are given in Appendix III.

The company must maintain a register of directors' interests (section 325) which must be available for inspection (Schedule 13, Part IV). Members may inspect the register free of charge; others may be charged a prescribed fee. The register must also be made available at the company's annual general meeting. The company is obliged to provide copies of the register on request, for a prescribed fee.

The interests in shares or debentures as recorded in the register of each person who is a director at the end of the financial year must be stated in the directors' report, or alternatively in the notes to the accounts (Schedule 7). Both the interests at the beginning of the year (or at the date of appointment) and at the end of the year must be disclosed. If a director has no interest, this must be stated. Duplicated holdings (for example, joint holdings) are counted as interests of each of the holders.

Disclosure must also be made with respect to each director of the number of shares in and amount of debentures of the company or group company in which rights to subscribe were either granted to or exercised during the year by, the director, his or her spouse or infant children. The numbers or amounts disclosed should be as recorded in the register.

If the company's shares or debentures are listed on a recognised investment exchange, the company must inform that investment exchange of changes in directors' interests (section 329).

Stock exchange companies are in addition required to disclose any options held by a director at the end of the year in the capital of any member of the group (*Admission of Securities to Listing* section 5, Chapter 2, paragraph 21(h)). Stock exchange companies are also required to distinguish between beneficial and non-beneficial interests. An interest should be shown as non-beneficial only if neither the director nor his spouse or infant children has any beneficial interest. Particulars should be given of the extent of any duplication which occurs. Stock Exchange companies must also disclose in the financial statements any changes in directors' interests or options which have occurred between the end of the financial year and a date not more than one month prior to the date of the notice of the meeting. If there has been no change, this fact must be disclosed.

4.32 Option dealings

It is a criminal offence for a director (or his spouse or infant children) to buy any kind of option in listed shares or debentures of a company of which he is a director, or of a company in the same group (section 323). However, it is not an offence for a director to:

(a) buy a right to subscribe for shares or debentures directly from the company;

(b) buy debentures that confer the right to subscribe for, or convert the debentures to, shares of the company.

The prohibition applies only to listed securities, so it does not apply to options in shares or debentures of a private company, or to unlisted securities of a public company.

A director for this purpose includes a shadow director.

4.40 INSIDER DEALING

A director buying or selling shares in his own company is clearly at an advantage over everybody else because of his inside knowledge. He might thus be expected to be precluded from exploiting this knowledge for personal gain.

However, in *Percival v Wright* (see paragraph 3.11, above), the directors were allowed to buy shares without disclosing an intended take-over offer because their actions did not damage the company, and it is the company to which directors owe their fiduciary duty.

Whether the same decision would be reached under modern conditions is not certain. The example of *Regal (Hastings) Ltd v Gulliver* (see paragraph 3.24, above) suggests that a profit arising through a director's connection with the company would be accountable to the company, although not to individual shareholders. However, this precedent may not extend to dealing in the company's shares.

There are two possible avenues for shareholders who have been victims of insider dealing. In *Percival v Wright* there was no suggestion of misrepresentation or unfair dealing by the directors, who were themselves approached by the shareholders wishing to sell. In other circumstances it might be possible to show fraud. Secondly, there is now also statutory protection in certain circumstances for shareholders whose interests have been unfairly prejudiced in the conduct of the company's affairs (section 459, see paragraph 7.44, below). Redress for insider dealing may be available under this section, although no cases have yet been before the courts.

4.41 Company Securities (Insider Dealing) Act 1985

Insider dealing is also, in certain circumstances, a criminal offence under the Companies Securities (Insider Dealing) Act 1985 (which contains the provisions first enacted in the Companies Act 1980). Conviction can bring a seven-year prison sentence or an unlimited fine or both. The Act is concerned only with dealings on a recognised stock exchange or a recognised investment exchange or with off-market deals in advertised securities and does not prohibit 'face to face' deals outside a recognised market. The Stock Exchange (including the Unlisted Securities Market), NASDAQ and OM London Ltd are recognised stock exchanges (Company Securities (Insider Dealing) Act 1985, section 16, SI 1989/2165 and SI 1990/47).

Since private companies' shares are not dealt through recognised markets they are largely unaffected by the Act. Similarly, the facts in *Percival v Wright* would not come within the scope of its provisions.

Although the Act creates a criminal offence for insider dealing, it does not enable the deal to be declared void or provide for compensation. It includes in its coverage:

(a) dealing by an insider;

(b) dealing as a so-called 'tippee'; that is, on the basis of information provided by an insider;

(c) 'counselling or procuring' someone else to deal on the basis of inside information;

(d) communicating insider information to someone likely to use it for the purpose of dealing.

Insiders are described in the Act as persons 'knowingly connected' with the company or another company in the same group. Directors are insiders by definition (Company Securities (Insider Dealing) Act 1985, section 9). Connected persons are defined also to include officers, employees and anyone else whose professional or business relationship with the company might be expected to provide access to unpublished price-sensitive information. They include virtually anyone who has lawful access to insider information such as auditors, bankers, solicitors and, specifically, public servants. The definition of an insider is broadened in the context of take-over bids to include anyone who is contemplating making an offer. For the purpose of the Act, a connection with the company extends back six months.

Unpublished price-sensitive information means specific matters relating to the company which, if they became known to dealers in the company's securities, would be likely to affect the price materially (Company Securities (Insider Dealing) Act 1985, section 10). Knowledge of general matters relating to the company does not fall within the scope of the Act.

Only transactions on a recognised stock exchange or in advertised securities through an off-market dealer are caught by the Act. Securities are 'advertised' if they are listed or their prices are published in some other way to facilitate dealing. An 'off-market' dealer is a dealer recognised under the Financial Services Act 1986, such as most merchant banks, licensed dealers and other recognised dealers such as members of FIMBRA.

The rules are complex and prosecutions have been rare. In order to convict an insider it is necessary to prove that the accused:

(a) was knowingly connected with the company;

(b) held information by virtue of his connection with that company;

(c) could reasonably have been expected by virtue of his position not to disclose such information (except for the proper performance of his job);

(d) knew that the information was unpublished, price-sensitive information;

(e) dealt in the company's securities through a recognised stock exchange (or, if they are advertised securities, through an off-market dealer).

Directors may find themselves receiving information from an insider, and thus in the position of a tippee. To convict a tippee it is necessary to show that he:

(a) knowingly obtained information, directly or indirectly, from someone connected with the company;

(b) knew, or had reasonable cause to believe, that the information was held by virtue of that connection;

(c) knew, or had reasonable cause to believe, that it would be reasonable for the tippee not to disclose the information except for the proper performance of his job;

(d) knew that the information was unpublished price-sensitive information;

(e) dealt in the company's securities through a recognised stock exchange (or, if they are advertised securities, through an off-market dealer).

In *A-G's Reference (No 1 of 1988)* [1989] AC 971, it was decided by the House of Lords that 'obtained' was intended to convey the general meaning of 'acquire' or 'get' and there was no need for the information to be actively sought out.

There are a number of defences under the Insider Dealing Act. The first allows an individual to deal in relevant securities – provided he is not using information to make a profit or to avoid a loss (Company Securities (Insider Dealing) Act 1985, section 3). What would succeed as a defence under this head is not clear; commentators have suggested that a forced sale of securities to meet a debt would be allowed since the motive for the sale is not to benefit from the inside information. The scope of the defence will have to be decided by the courts. In *R v Cross* [1990] BCC 237 it was stated that this defence was a matter to be established by a defendant, it was not necessary for a prosecution to disprove the defence to establish a case.

Insolvency practitioners are exempted from the prohibitions in relation to transactions carried out in the course of their duties. A similar exemption applies to stock jobbers and market makers (in securities).

A further defence allows an individual whose knowledge of a particular transaction gives him unpublished price-sensitive information to proceed nevertheless with the transaction. A practical effect of this appears to be to allow someone contemplating a take-over to continue to buy shares in the market.

4.42 Non-statutory codes

While the Stock Exchange considers it desirable that directors of listed companies should hold securities in their companies it realises that special considerations apply to their dealings. It has therefore formulated a model code that goes beyond that required by legislation. Listed companies must adopt rules governing directors' dealings which are no less exacting than this model code (*Admission of Securities to Listing* section 5, Chapter 2, paragraph 44). The model code seeks to address both the situation where a director is unaware of a price-sensitive matter and should be told not to deal and also dealing in the periods prior to a regular announcement or a price-sensitive announcement. The Code includes rules prohibiting directors from dealing:

(a) on a short-term basis;

(b) when in possession of unpublished, price-sensitive information;

(c) during the two months prior to the publication of interim or final results, except for a sale in exceptional circumstances.

Employees and persons connected with directors are also affected in certain circumstances. The full text of the model code is reproduced in Appendix VIII.

The City Code on Take-overs and Mergers prohibits dealings in a company's securities by anyone who has confidential price-sensitive information concerning an offer or contemplated offer for the company (The City Code on Take-overs and Mergers, Section E, rule 4).

The Institute of Directors has an advisory Code of Conduct on Insider Dealing. Its rules are similar to those of the Company Securities (Insider Dealing) Act 1985 but are intended to have a much wider application.

4.50 DISCLOSURE

All the information dealt with in the following paragraphs is also required from shadow directors: that is, persons in accordance with whose directions or instructions the directors are accustomed to act (see paragraph 1.11, above).

4.51 Register of directors and secretaries

Section 288 requires every company to maintain a register of directors and secretaries. In the case of a director it must show (section 289):

(a) his name, address and nationality;

(b) any former name;

(c) his business occupation;

(d) particulars of other directorships held at any time in the past five years;

(e) his date of birth.

The name must include a forename and surname and the address must be the usual residential address. The requirement to disclose other directorships does not apply in respect of dormant companies or companies 'grouped with' the company keeping the register. A company is grouped with another if it is its wholly-owned subsidiary or holding company or they are both wholly-owned subsidiaries of another.

If the director is a corporation (which includes a company registered in Great Britain or elsewhere) it must show its corporate name and registered or principal office.

Any change in the directors or in the details contained in the register must be notified to the registrar (on Form 288) within 14 days. The register must be kept at the registered office and be available for inspection by members free of charge and by others on payment of the prescribed fee.

The disclosure requirement for company secretaries is less stringent, amounting only to name, any former name and usual residential address (section 290).

4.52 Directors' names on company correspondence

A company's business letters must not contain a director's name (except in the text or as signatory) unless the names of all the directors are shown (section 305).

4.53 Inspection of service contracts

Every company must make available for inspection a copy of each director's service contract; or, if the contract is not in writing, a memorandum setting out its terms (section 318).

All the documents must be kept at the registered office, or the place where the register of members is kept if different, or at its principal place of business in England and Wales or Scotland, depending on where it is registered. They must be available for inspection free of charge by any member of the company.

The company must also make available copies of service contracts of each director employed by a subsidiary.

Section 318 enables members to gauge the potential cost of dismissing a director by calculating the amount remaining under his service contract. Where the contract has less than 12 months to run or if it can be terminated within the next 12 months without payment of compensation, the company is not required to keep copies for inspection.

Under section 319 a director's contract of employment can only exceed five years subject to certain conditions. This is discussed more fully in Chapter 9.

4.54 Documents available for inspection

The directors are required to make certain documents available for inspection:

(a) *Register of members* Every company must maintain a register giving particulars (including names and addresses and shareholdings) of members (section 352). This must be open for inspection (section 356).

(b) *Register of debenture holders* There is no statutory requirement to keep such a register, but if there is one, section 191 confers the right of members and others to inspect it.

(c) *Minutes of general meetings* Every company must keep books containing the minutes of all general meetings, directors' meetings and meetings of managers (section 382). Minutes of general meetings must be made available for inspection under section 383.

(d) *Register of directors and secretaries* (section 288, see paragraph 4.51, above).

(e) *Directors' service contracts* (section 318, see paragraph 4.53, above).

(f) *Register of director's interests in shares and debentures* (section 324, see paragraph 4.31, above).

(g) *Register of charges* Every company must maintain a register showing particulars of all charges on its property and those entitled to them (section 422). The register and copies of the instruments creating the charges must be made available for inspection (section 423). (These requirements will be contained in sections 411 and 412 once the amendments contained in Part IV of the Companies Act 1989 take effect.)

(h) *Register of interests in shares* Holders of substantial interests (3% or more) in the shares of public companies must notify the company of their holdings and changes thereto (section 198). Under section 211 every company must maintain a register of substantial interests which must be made available for inspection (section 219).

4.55 Annual return

Every company must file with the registrar an annual return signed by a director or the secretary (section 363). The return must be completed within 28 days of the 'return date', and must contain the information prescribed on Form 363 regarding the address of the registered office, names and holdings of past and present shareholders, details of share capital, the type of company and its principal business activities, whether the company has passed certain elective resolutions, and particulars of directors and secretaries.

A company's 'return date' is:

(a) the anniversary of the company's incorporation; or

(b) if the company's last return was made up to a different date, the anniversary of that date.

4.60 APPOINTMENT OF COMPANY SECRETARY

Every company must have a secretary (section 283). A sole director may not also be secretary. It is the duty of the directors of a public company (under section 286) to take all reasonable steps to secure that the secretary 'is a person who appears to them to have the requisite knowledge and experience to discharge the functions of secretary', and who:

(a) was secretary or assistant or deputy secretary of the company on 22 December 1980 (when this provision came into force); or

(b) for at least three of the five years immediately preceding his appointment as secretary held the office of secretary of a company other than a private company; or

(c) is a member of any of these professional bodies:

the Institute of Chartered Accountants in England and Wales;
the Institute of Chartered Accountants of Scotland;
the Chartered Association of Certified Accountants;
the Institute of Chartered Accountants in Ireland;
the Institute of Chartered Secretaries and Administrators;
the Institute of Cost and Management Accountants;
the Chartered Institute of Public Finance and Accountancy; or

(d) is a barrister, advocate or solicitor; or

(e) is a person who, by virtue of his holding or having held any other position or his being a member of any other body, appears to the directors to be capable of discharging those functions.

4.70 DEPARTMENT OF TRADE AND INDUSTRY INVESTIGATIONS

Directors have a statutory duty to co-operate in an investigation of the company by the Department of Trade and Industry. Obstructing formally appointed inspectors is contempt of court, punishable at the court's discretion. Failure to co-operate in other investigations is punishable by a fine.

4.71 Investigation of the company's affairs

The Secretary of State for Trade and Industry must appoint inspectors to investigate the affairs of the company if ordered to do so by the court. He also has discretion to do so in the following circumstances:

(a) on the application of the company or a prescribed minority of members (section 431);

(b) if the company's affairs have been conducted with the intention of defrauding creditors or for some other fraudulent or unlawful purpose;

(c) if the company was formed for a fraudulent or unlawful purpose;

(d) if the promoters or officers have been guilty of fraud, misfeasance or other misconduct towards the company's members; or

(e) if the company's members have not been given all the information they might reasonably expect (section 432).

All agents and officers of the company are obliged to give the inspectors all the assistance they are reasonably able to give, which includes producing all the company's documents and attending before the inspectors when required (section 434).

The inspectors can require any person they believe to be in possession of information relating to an investigation to produce documents, including those not in a legible form, attend before the inspectors or otherwise to assist the inspectors (section 434). The inspectors' powers were increased to this level by the Companies Act 1989.

An officer or agent who refuses to co-operate with the inspectors and anyone who refuses to answer a question put to them by the inspectors for the purpose of the investigation is guilty of contempt of court (section 436), and his punishment is at the discretion of the court.

4.72 Requisition and seizure of documents

The Secretary of State may at any time direct a company to produce its documents for inspection if he thinks there is good reason (section 447). The power includes the right to copy documents and to demand explanations from past or present officers or employees. There is also a right to obtain a warrant to enter and search the company's premises (section 448). These investigative powers can be exercised without appointing inspectors, enabling enquiries to be carried out with a minimum of publicity. Anyone failing to co-operate is liable to a fine.

4.73 Investigation of ownership and share dealings

The Secretary of State has the power to appoint inspectors to investigate the true ownership and control of a company if it appears that there is good reason to do so (section 442). There is a mandatory duty to do so if the prescribed minimum of members request it, unless the request is vexatious.

The Secretary of State may also carry out an investigation to establish whether there have been breaches of the regulations concerning directors' share dealings or of the duty of directors to notify interests in shares and debentures (section 446).

4.74 Investigation into insider dealing

If it appears to the Secretary of State that there may have been a contravention of the Company Securities (Insider Dealing) Act 1985 he may appoint inspectors to establish whether any such contravention has occurred (Financial Services Act 1986, section 177). While the powers of the inspectors are similar to those under the Companies Act, the consequences of non-co-operation are slightly greater. The powers of the inspectors under this section were tested in *Re an Inquiry under the Company Securities (Insider Dealing) Act 1985* (1987) 4 BCC 35 when it was held that a journalist had no reasonable excuse for failing to comply with an inspector's request for information. On receipt of the inspector's report, the Secretary of State may apply for a disqualification order against a director (see paragraph 1.33, above).

5 Accounting responsibilities of directors

The company's annual report and accounts are the means by which the members gauge how well the directors have managed the company's assets entrusted to their care. It is specifically the duty of the directors – not the company – to prepare and present accounts. Where a company is the parent of a group the directors must also present accounts for the group as a whole in the form of consolidated accounts. The statutory rules are strict, to ensure that the directors' account is true and fair and discloses at least a basic minimum of information.

The Companies Act requires that proper accounting records are kept, specifies the form and content of the annual accounts, and provides for an annual independent audit. There are also rules requiring the presentation of the accounts to members and governing their publication.

Although the accounts are principally a duty owed by the directors to the shareholders, they are used by many other individuals, including potential investors, lenders, trade creditors, customers and employees, as well as various arms of government. They are therefore an important link between the company and outsiders, and directors should carry out their accounting responsibilities with that in mind.

5.10 ACCOUNTING RECORDS

5.11 Contents

The company must keep sufficient accounting records:

(a) to show and explain the company's transactions;

(b) to disclose the company's financial position with reasonable accuracy at any time; and

(c) to enable the directors to ensure that any balance sheet and profit and loss account they are required to prepare comply with the Act (section 221).

In particular, accounting records must contain:

(a) entries from day to day of all sums of money received and expended and the matters in respect of which the receipts and expenditure take place;

(b) a record of the assets and liabilities of the company; and

(c) where the company's business involves dealing in goods;

  (i) statements of stock held at the end of each financial year;

  (ii) all statements of stocktaking from which any statements in (i) above have been prepared; and

  (iii) except in the case of goods sold by way of ordinary retail trade, statements of all goods sold and purchased, in sufficient detail to identify the goods and the buyers and sellers.

A parent company which has a subsidiary undertaking must take reasonable steps to ensure that the undertaking keeps adequate accounting records even if there are no legal requirements for it to do so. The accounting records must be sufficient to enable the directors of the parent company to ensure that the parent's individual and group accounts comply with the Act (section 221).

5.12 Meaning

The Institute of Chartered Accountants in England and Wales has obtained counsel's opinion on some of the points of difficulty arising from section 221 dealing with accounting records. It is expected that a guidance statement will be issued in the latter part of 1991. The following points are drawn from a final draft of the statement:

(a) The accounting records should be such as would allow the directors to prepare a reasonably accurate statement of the company's financial position at any time. They need not contain the additional information that may be required to make the accounts true and fair. However, the financial position is not limited to the cash position. It includes the assets and liabilities including depreciation, bad debts and other losses. Clearly this requires a company's stock position to be assessible at any time, but does not require the accuracy of a stocktake.

(b) The requirement that accounting records should be capable of showing the financial position at any time does not mean that they should be updated instantaneously, but that transactions should be recorded in a reasonable time.

(c) It follows that accounting records should comprise an orderly, classified collection of information; not an unorganised collection of vouchers and documents.

The records can be in any form the company chooses, including computerised and other non-legible forms so long as they can be reproduced in legible form (sections 722, 723).

5.13 Retention of records

The accounting records may be kept wherever the directors think fit. They must at all times be open to inspection by the company's officers, so a director cannot be denied access to them (section 222).

A private company must retain its accounting records for three years, and a public company for six years (section 222). However, it is usual to retain records for as long as they may be required for tax or other legal purposes. Under the Limitation Act 1980 the following are the periods within which an action can be brought:

(a) in the case of a simple contract, six years from the date on which the cause of action arose (section 5);

(b) in the case of a contract under seal (specialty contract), 12 years (section 8);

(c) in actions for tort, six years from when the damage occurred (section 2) or, where the claim is for the tort of negligence, but is not in respect of personal injury or death, three years from the date that the damage was discoverable if the plaintiff prefers. This latter period (three years from discoverability) is subject to a 15-year 'longshop' (no action can be brought more than 15 years after the tort occurred);

(d) in the special case of personal injury, three years from the date on which the cause of action became apparent (section 11).

There are also requirements to produce documents for the tax authorities. The Inland Revenue normally has power to raise tax assessments for up to six years after the event (Taxes Management Act 1970, section 34). However, assessments may be raised at any time in the case of the taxpayer's fraud or neglect (Taxes Management Act 1970, sections 36 and 39).

If registered for VAT, the company must keep records and accounts and related documents for six years (Finance Act 1985, Schedule 7, paragraph 2).

Employers must retain Pay As You Earn records for three years (Income Tax (Employments) Regulations 1973 as amended, regulation 32(5)); they must also retain records of National Insurance Contributions for three years (Social Security (Contributions) Regulations 1979 as amended, Schedule 1, paragraph 32(5)).

Copies of the original documents are admissible in court so long as they can be relied upon as accurate. A judge has power under section 6 of the Civil Evidence Act 1968 to admit copies in court and to specify the method of authentication. When transferring records to microfilm, it is good practice for directors to establish procedures to ensure that all records are copied and authenticated as true copies and safely stored. Where accounting records are in a non-legible form any software etc necessary to retrieve the records in a usable form should also be retained.

5.14 False accounting

False accounting is a criminal offence under section 17 of the Theft Act 1968. It describes circumstances in which a person dishonestly, with a view to gain for himself or another, or with intent to cause loss to another:

(a) destroys, defaces, conceals or falsifies any account or any record or document made or required for any accounting purpose; or

(b) in furnishing information for any purpose produces or makes use of any account, or any such record or document as aforesaid, which to his knowledge is or may be misleading, false or deceptive in material particular.

If a director consents to or connives in the commission of such an offence by the company he is himself liable to imprisonment for up to seven years (Theft Act 1968, section 18).

5.20 ANNUAL ACCOUNTS

The directors of every UK company registered under the Companies Acts (including an unlimited company) are required by section 241 to lay before the company in general meeting the annual accounts, directors' report and the auditor's report on those accounts in respect of each financial year. The accounts must comply with the requirements of the Act as to form and content. In particular they must give a true and fair view of the company's state of affairs and of its profit for the year (see paragraph 5.31, below).

Private companies may elect to dispense with laying accounts and reports at a general meeting (see paragraph 7.30, below).

The Act defines 'annual accounts' as including the individual company and/or consolidated balance sheets, profit and loss accounts and the information required or allowed to be disclosed in the notes thereto (sections 261 and 262). But the parent company's individual profit and loss account is not required to be published or filed where group accounts are prepared (see paragraph 5.34, below).

The accountancy bodies have adopted the term 'financial statements' to refer to the various separate items, including notes to the accounts, that are intended collectively to give a true and fair view. The term 'accounts' is not formally defined but is usually used to refer to the formal accounting statements, that is, profit and loss accounts and balance sheets (and statement of source and application of funds or cash flow statement, where applicable).

The balance sheet must be signed by a director on behalf of the board. The board must approve the annual accounts before the balance sheet is signed (section 233). Copies of the annual accounts and reports must then be sent to every member and debenture holder not less than 21 days before the date of the annual general meeting (section 238). In addition, unless the company is unlimited, it must deliver a copy of these documents to the registrar within ten months (seven months for a public company) of the end of the accounting reference period (sections 242 and 244). Companies listed on The

Stock Exchange must issue their reports and annual accounts within six months of the year end.

In certain cases, small and medium-sized companies may opt to prepare condensed versions of their financial statements solely for the purpose of filing with the registrar. This subject is discussed in paragraph 5.62, below.

5.21 True and fair view

Financial statements are required to give a true and fair view of the profit or loss for the financial year and of the state of affairs at the end of it. This requirement overrides all the accounting requirements of the Act and FRSs. If the information specified by the Act is not sufficient to give a true and fair view, the additional information must be given (sections 226 and 227).

5.30 FORM AND CONTENT OF ANNUAL ACCOUNTS

5.31 Schedule 4

With the exception of special category companies (see paragraph 5.35, below), annual accounts must comply with the requirements of the Fourth Schedule to the Companies Act.

A company is required to choose from two balance sheet formats and four profit and loss account formats set out in Schedule 4. Balance sheet format 1 and profit and loss account formats 1 and 2 follow the vertical arrangement of items and are customarily adopted in the UK. (The alternative formats place the same items in a double-sided, or horizontal, arrangement.) The profit and loss account formats offer the further choice of analysing costs by type of operation (sales, distribution etc) or type of expenditure (raw materials, staff costs etc). The formats chosen cannot be changed unless in the opinion of the directors there are special reasons for a change. A note to the accounts would then be required, giving particulars for the change of format and explaining the reasons for it (Schedule 4, paragraph 2).

The individual items making up one format are allocated letters, Roman numerals and Arabic numerals in Schedule 4. These designations do not appear in the financial statements, but dictate the order in which the individual items must appear in the financial statements (although items which have been allocated Arabic numerals may be adapted or rearranged in certain circumstances).

5.32 Fundamental accounting principles

Financial statements must be prepared on the basis of five fundamental accounting principles laid down in Schedule 4, paragraphs 10 to 14.

(a) *Going concern* The company must be presumed to be carrying on business as a going concern, which assumes that it will continue its operations into the foreseeable future with no significant reduction in the scale of operations.

(b) *Consistency* Accounting policies must be applied consistently within the same accounts and from one financial year to the next.

(c) *Prudence* The amount of any item must be determined on a prudent basis, so:

   (i) only profits realised at the balance sheet date may be included in the profit and loss account;

   (ii) all liabilities and losses which have arisen or are liable to arise in respect of any period prior to the balance sheet date must be taken into account (including all those which become apparent before the balance sheet is signed on behalf of the directors).

(d) *Accruals* Income or charges relating to the financial year must be taken into account without regard to the date of receipt or payment.

(e) *Separate determination of items* When determining the aggregate amount of any item, the amount of each individual asset or liability included in it must be determined separately.

5.33 Other rules as to form and content

Schedule 4 sets out a number of other general rules governing the form and content of the accounts. These include:

(a) *Corresponding amounts* Figures for the preceding year must be shown to correspond with all the items in the accounts and, with certain exceptions, the notes to the accounts. The figures must be comparable between the two years, and any adjustment to achieve comparability must be disclosed and explained.

(b) *Greater detail* Any item may be shown in greater detail than required by the format, in which case it is good practice to provide a sub-total. Greater detail must be given if it is necessary in order to give a true and fair view.

(c) *Headings* A heading should be omitted if there is no amount to be included under it in either the preceding or the current year. Additional headings are permissible where an item is not covered by the existing headings.

(d) *Offsets* Assets and income may not be set off against liabilities and expenditure.

(e) *Immaterial amounts* Any amount which in the context of Schedule 4 is not material need not be disclosed separately. Whether an amount is or is not material should be judged by reference to the needs of the users of the financial statements.

5.34 Group accounts

Section 227 requires any company which has subsidiary undertakings at the end of its financial year, ie a parent company, to produce group accounts in the form of consolidated accounts. The parent company's balance sheet must also be given. While the parent company must draw up a profit and loss account and the board of directors must approve it, it need not be published or filed, nor do the notes to the profit and loss account otherwise required by Schedule 4 need to be drawn up, provided certain disclosures are made (section 230).

Small and medium-sized groups are exempt from the requirement to produce group accounts (see paragraph 5.62, below).

Provided it does not have any of its securities listed on an EC Stock Exchange and it complies with certain other conditions (section 228), a parent company is not required to prepare group accounts if it is itself a wholly-owned subsidiary undertaking and its immediate parent undertaking is established under the law of a member state of the European Community (an EC parent).

Additionally, a company which is not wholly-owned and is not listed need not prepare group accounts if:

(a) the immediate EC parent holds more than 50% of its shares; and

(b) there has been no notice served on the company by outside shareholders holding in aggregate either more than half of its remaining shares or 5% of its total shares, requesting the preparation of group accounts. The notice must be served at least six months before the end of the financial year to which it relates.

One of the conditions that must be complied with is that the company must deliver to the registrar, within the period allowed for delivering its individual accounts, a copy in English of the parent's group accounts and directors' report and the audit report thereon. Section 229 also sets out certain circumstances in which a subsidiary may be excluded from consolidation provided certain disclosures are made.

5.35 Special category companies

Banking and insurance companies may comply with the lesser requirements of Schedule 9 instead of with Schedule 4 (section 255).

A banking company means a company authorised under the Banking Act 1987. An insurance company is one to which Part II of the Insurance Companies Act 1982 applies.

5.36 Financial Reporting Standards

Financial Reporting Standards (FRSs) are issued by the Accounting Standards Board (ASB), a body authorised to issue 'Accounting Standards' for the purposes of section 256. The ASB has adopted the 22 Statements of Standard Accounting Practice (SSAPs) extant at 1 August 1990 as FRSs and is in the process of developing further standards and amendments to existing standards which it will issue from time to time.

The SSAPs were issued by the UK accounting bodies and prepared by the Accounting Standards Committee, now replaced by the ASB.

Directors of companies, other than small and medium-sized companies (see paragraph 5.62, below), are required to disclose particulars of any non-compliance with applicable FRSs in their financial statements (Schedule 4, paragraph 36A and section 246). Unless the auditor concurs with a significant departure he is required to qualify his report.

Companies listed on The Stock Exchange are specifically required to comply with accounting standards.

The ASB has set up an Urgent Issues Task Force (UITF). The UITF's main role is to assist in areas where an accounting standard or Companies Act provision exists but where unsatisfactory or conflicting interpretations have developed or seem likely to develop. The UITF will seek to obtain a consensus on the issue in question. While the concensus will not have the status of an accounting standard, the Review Panel may take it into account in considering whether financial statements require revision (see paragraph 5.66, below).

5.40 THE DIRECTORS' REPORT

For each financial year the directors must prepare a report containing certain specified information. The required information is set out in section 234 and in Schedule 7 and summarised in Appendix VI. The matters required by The Stock Exchange to be disclosed by listed companies are also usually included in the directors' report. In the case of a holding company the report must take account of the whole group.

The report must be approved by the board of directors and signed on behalf of the board by a director or the secretary of the company (section 234A).

5.50 RELATIONSHIP WITH AUDITORS

5.51 The auditors' report

Auditors are required to report to the members of the company on every balance sheet and profit and loss account and on all group accounts laid before the members in general meeting during their terms of office (section 235). They are required to state whether in their opinion the balance sheet, profit and loss account and group accounts give a true and fair view of the state of affairs and profit or loss for the year, and whether in their opinion the accounts have been properly prepared in accordance with the Act.

The auditors have a duty under sections 235 and 237 to carry out such investigations as will enable them to form an opinion as to whether or not:

(a) proper accounting records have been kept by the company and proper returns adequate for their audit have been received from branches which they did not visit;

(b) the balance sheet and profit and loss account are in agreement with the accounting records (and returns); and

(c) the information given in the directors' report is consistent with the financial statements.

The auditors must report specifically on these matters only if in their opinion the requirements have not been complied with. They must also report if they have not obtained all the information and explanations they require. The absence of any comment in their report is therefore equivalent to an assurance that they have satisfied themselves on these matters.

5.52 Appointment and removal of auditors

The directors appoint the first auditors of a company (sections 385 and 385A) or fill a casual vacancy in the office of auditor (section 388). Normally auditors must be appointed at each general meeting before which accounts are laid, to hold office until the conclusion of the next such meeting (section 385). They may be replaced or reappointed at this meeting.

In the case of a private company that has elected not to lay accounts (see paragraph 7.30, below) and where no notice requiring accounts to be laid has been given the auditors must be appointed at a general meeting or by written resolution (see paragraph 7.32, below) before the end of a period of 28 days beginning when the financial statements for the previous financial year are sent to members (section 385A). Auditors of a private company are deemed to be reappointed each year if an elective resolution not to reappoint auditors annually is in force (section 386, see paragraph 7.30, below).

The auditors may resign or be removed before the expiry of their term of office (sections 391, 392 and 393). When an auditor ceases to hold office for any reason, he must send a statement to the company's registered office that there are no circumstances connected with his ceasing to hold office that need to be brought to the attention of members or creditors, or a statement of such circumstances if there are any. If there are such circumstances, the company must circulate a copy of the statement to members and anyone else entitled to receive the company's accounts. However, the company may ask the court to intervene if it considers that the statement is being used to secure needless publicity for defamatory matter (section 394). In addition, auditors who wish to explain the circumstances connected with their resignation may require the directors to convene an extraordinary general meeting to receive and consider the explanation (section 392A). A resigning auditor must send a notice of resignation to the company in addition to the statement of circumstances. A notice of resignation must be filed with the registrar by the company within 14 days and the statement of circumstances filed with the registrar by the auditor.

Before accepting an appointment, auditors are required by their ethical rules to request of the auditor last appointed all information which ought to be made available to them to enable them to decide whether they are prepared to accept nomination.

The Secretary of State must be notified within one week of the end of the period for appointing auditors if the company fails to appoint or reappoint an auditor. The company and every officer who is in default is liable to a fine if such notice is not given (section 387).

5.53 Rights of auditors

Auditors have the right to attend all general meetings and to speak on any business which concerns them as auditors (section 390). They are not entitled to attend meetings of the board or management, but they are often invited to attend the board meeting at which the accounts are approved.

Every auditor has a right of access at all times to the company's books, accounts and vouchers and is entitled to require from the company's officers whatever information or explanations he thinks necessary for the performance of his duties as auditor (section 389A). The auditor need not explain his reasons for requesting any particular information. It is a criminal offence for a director (or any other officer) knowingly to make a false or misleading statement to the auditor (section 389A).

Section 389A imposes a duty on subsidiary undertakings that are bodies corporate incorporated in Great Britain and their auditors to give the holding company auditors any information and explanations they may reasonably require. A parent company has a duty to take such steps as are reasonably open to it to obtain such information and explanations from a subsidiary undertaking that is not a body corporate incorporated in Great Britain.

The statutory rights of auditors cannot be restricted in any way (*Newton v Birmingham Small Arms Co Ltd* [1906] 2 Ch 378). Any attempt to limit the liability of auditors is void under section 310 save as provided by that section (see paragraph 3.10, above).

5.54 Communication with the auditors

There are three formal communications often made between the directors and the auditor:

(a) *Letter of engagement* Before the start of the audit the auditor and the company should agree in writing the extent of the auditor's responsibilities. This minimises the possibility of any misunderstanding. Typically, the letter will outline the legal requirements relating to the audit and emphasise that the directors are responsible for maintaining the accounting records and preparing the accounts. It will also point out that the audit should not be relied on to expose fraud. Where the auditor has been requested to provide additional services, such as preparing draft accounts or tax computations, the letter will clearly separate this work from the statutory audit.

(b) *Report to management* The auditor will normally write to the company commenting on the accounting records, systems and controls he has examined during the audit. He will bring to management's attention any weaknesses which he has found in systems that might lead to material errors, and may make recommendations for improvement. The directors should ensure that all recommendations are properly considered, and taken up if considered appropriate.

(c) *Letter of representation* The auditor has a duty to obtain independent evidence to support his opinion on the financial statements. However, in certain circumstances, such as where knowledge of the facts is confined to management or where the matter is principally one of judgement and opinion, the auditor may have to rely on representations by management which are unsupported by corroborative evidence. In such cases the auditor will normally require a letter from the board setting out the matters on which he has received only uncorroborated representations by management. In signing such a letter the board accepts responsibility for its contents, but does not reduce the auditor's ultimate responsibility for his opinion.

5.55 Audit committees

The auditor's primary duty is to the shareholders, to whom his statutory report is addressed. It is therefore important that he remains independent of management, and large companies may find it useful to set up a separate committee of the board to liaise directly with the auditor. The tasks of this 'audit committee' include assuring itself that any disagreements between the auditor and management have been properly resolved and that the audit has been completed satisfactorily. The committee is also usually expected to review the company's financial statements and to monitor the effectiveness of its system of internal control, with particular regard to the auditor's advice and recommendations. To make the audit committee as free as possible from management influence it usually has a majority of non-executive directors, and no members with executive responsibility for accounting or finance. However, the structure and responsibilities of the audit committee vary from company to company in accordance with particular needs and circumstances.

5.60 FILING AND PUBLICATION OF ACCOUNTS

5.61 Accounting reference periods

The Act requires the directors to prepare annual accounts for the company's financial year (sections 226 and 227). This normally coincides with the accounting reference period but in order to accommodate 52-week accounting, the financial year may vary by seven days either way (section 223). The accounting reference period ends on the accounting reference date, which must be notified to the registrar within nine months of incorporation or is, by default, the anniversary of the last day of the month of incorporation. The first accounting reference period must be between six and 18 months, commencing on the date of incorporation (not of trading) (section 224).

Succeeding accounting reference periods normally last 12 months, but may be changed subject to certain conditions (see Appendix II).

5.62 Modified accounts

In most cases the accounts to be delivered to the registrar will be the same as those required by section 241 to be laid before the company in general meeting. However, certain companies which qualify as small or medium-sized may take advantage of the exemptions given in sections 246 to 249 and file 'modified' accounts with the registrar. (The term 'modified accounts' is no longer used in the Act as a consequence of amendments made by the Companies Act 1989. We have continued to use the term in this book for convenience.) Although modified accounts disclose less information than full accounts they require the production of another set of financial statements solely for this purpose, and not all companies consider it worthwhile.

A small company is one which satisfies two or more of the following conditions:

(a) turnover not exceeding £2,000,000;

(b) balance sheet total not exceeding £975,000;

(c) average number of employees not exceeding 50.

A medium-sized company is one which satisfies two or more of the following conditions:

(a) turnover not exceeding £8,000,000;

(b) balance sheet total not exceeding £3,900,000;

(c) average number of employees not exceeding 250.

The balance sheet total is the total of all assets without any deduction for liabilities.

In both cases the conditions must be satisfied in respect of the financial year for which modified accounts are to be filed and the immediately preceding financial year. However, companies are allowed one year in which the criteria are exceeded before their status changes. Public companies, and banking and insurance companies may not file modified accounts, regardless of their size; nor may any company which is a member of a group which includes any such company.

A parent company can only qualify as a small company in relation to a financial year if the group headed by it qualifies as a small group, and can only qualify as a medium-sized company in a financial year if the group qualifies as a medium-sized group (section 246).

A small group is one which satisfies two or more of the following conditions:

(a) turnover not exceeding £2,000,000 net or £2,400,000 gross;

(b) balance sheet total not exceeding £1,000,000 net or £1,200,000 gross;

(c) average number of employees not exceeding 50.

A medium group is a group which satisfies two or more of the following conditions:

(a) turnover not exceeding £8,000,000 net or £9,600,000 gross;

(b) balance sheet total not exceeding £3,900,000 net or £4,700,000 gross;

(c) average number of employees not exceeding 250.

The figures for groups must be calculated in the same manner described above for companies. In the group figures, 'net' means with set-off and other adjustments required by Schedule 4A (ie elimination of intra-group turnover, balances and profits or losses), and 'gross' means without those set-offs and other adjustments. A group may satisfy the relevant requirements on the basis of either the net or the gross figure.

A small company qualifies for particularly wide exemptions, needing to file only a modified balance sheet and certain notes. A medium-sized company must file almost its full accounts, being exempt only from disclosing certain profit and loss account information regarding the make-up of profit before tax and certain notes. Small and medium-sized companies are exempt from the requirement to disclose non-compliance with accounting standards in both their modified accounts and in the full accounts sent to members (see paragraph 5.36, above).

The balance sheet included in modified accounts must contain a statement by the directors that they have relied on the exemptions. There must also be a special report by the auditors which, in addition to reproducing the full audit report, states that they are satisfied that the qualifying conditions are met.

Modified group accounts do not have to be prepared as small or medium-sized groups are exempt from the requirement to prepare group accounts (section 248).

5.63 Dormant companies

A company is dormant when it has no significant accounting transactions – that is, transactions required by section 221 to be entered in the company's accounting records (other than the taking up of shares in the memorandum). Thus a company is not dormant during a period in which it makes any payment or receives any sum of money, however small.

A dormant company may pass a special resolution exempting itself from the obligation to appoint auditors, subject to the following conditions (section 250):

(a) the resolution must be passed at a general meeting at which audited accounts for a financial year are laid (audited accounts need not be laid if the company has been dormant since incorporation);

(b) the company must qualify as a small company in that year;

(c) the directors are not required to lay group accounts in respect of the financial year;

(d) the company has been dormant since the year end.

5.64 Publication of accounts

Where a company publishes non-statutory accounts, that is, publishes any balance sheet or profit and loss account in respect of a financial year otherwise than as part of the statutory accounts, it must state that they are not statutory accounts (section 240). The statement must also say whether statutory accounts have been filed with the registrar, whether the auditors have reported on the statutory accounts and, if so, whether their report was qualified or contained any reservations about accounting records or obtaining necessary information.

Preliminary announcements of annual results and employee reports containing accounting information are the usual examples of non-statutory accounts. Interim figures which deal with only part of a financial year are not subject to the above requirements unless they contain information in respect of a full period as a comparative.

When statutory accounts are published they must always contain the auditors' report (section 240). Statutory accounts comprise individual or group accounts, or modified accounts (see paragraph 5.62, above).

5.65 Summary financial statements

Companies listed on the International Stock Exchange may send a shareholder a summary financial statement instead of the full financial statements if it has obtained the shareholder's consent and provided the company's articles do not require the full financial statements to be sent to members (section 251 and the Companies (Summary Financial Statements) Regulations 1990 SI 1990/515).

A shareholder gives his consent:

(a) if he notifies the company in writing that he wishes to receive a summary financial statement instead of the full financial statements and does not subsequently countermand the instruction; or

(b) if he fails to reply to a notice from the company inviting him to elect to receive summary financial statements, provided that several requirements have been observed, particularly the inclusion with that notice of both full and summary financial statements for a financial year preceding that for which the election is invited.

Also, when a summary financial statement is sent to members it must be accompanied by a reply paid card enabling them to request in addition the full financial statements for that and/or future financial years.

The form and content of a summary financial statement is specified by the Companies (Summary Financial Statements) Regulations 1990. The statement must:

(a) state that it is only a summary of information in the company's annual accounts and directors' report;

(b) contain an auditor's opinion as to consistency with the annual accounts and directors' report and compliance with the legislation;

(c) state whether the auditors' report on the annual accounts was unqualified or qualified: if qualified, the statement should set out the auditor's report in full together with any further material needed to understand the qualification; and

(d) state whether the auditors' report on the annual accounts contained any reservations about accounting records or obtaining necessary information and, if so, set them out in full.

5.66 Defective accounts

Following amendment by the Companies Act 1989, the Act for the first time provides for the revision of annual accounts and directors' reports which are defective insofar as they do not comply with the statutory requirements. In summary, the Act provides for:

(a) the directors voluntarily to amend the annual accounts or directors' report (section 245);

(b) the Secretary of State to request directors either to amend the annual accounts or directors' report or to explain the apparent non-compliance (section 245A); and

(c) the Secretary of State, or another person authorised for the purpose, to apply for a court order requiring directors to amend the annual accounts or directors' report (sections 245B and 245C).

The Companies (Revision of Defective Accounts and Report) Regulations 1990 (SI 1990/2570) set out how the provisions of the Act are to be applied to annual accounts or directors' reports that are being voluntarily revised because the originals do not comply with statutory requirements. In summary, they provide for:

(a) either a full revision, or for a partial revision by means of a supplementary note;

(b) the revised accounts or revised directors' report to be prepared as at the date of the approval of the original, defective, accounts or directors' report;

(c) specified statements to be made by the directors;

(d) the approval and signing of the revised accounts or report;

(e) an auditor's report on the revised accounts or report to be included;

(f) the steps to be taken with regard to revised accounts or revised reports where copies of the original, defective, accounts or report have been sent to members, laid before the company or delivered to the registrar.

The Review Panel of the Financial Reporting Council has been approved under section 245B for the purposes of challenging accounts as defective in the courts. If the court finds that the accounts are defective, it may order that all or part of the costs of the application and of the preparation of revised accounts shall be borne by the directors who were party to the approval of the defective accounts. For this purpose, every director of the company at the time the accounts were approved is taken to have been a party to their approval unless he shows that he took all reasonable steps to prevent their being approved.

6 Financial responsibilities of directors

One of the board's most important responsibilities is to manage the company's finances. At one level this presents directors with no more than a particular instance of their general duty to exercise skill and care. However, the wrongful trading provisions of the Insolvency Act 1986 (see Chapter 11) impose an additional burden by requiring a director to take every step to minimise the potential loss to creditors once he knows the company has no reasonable prospect of avoiding insolvent liquidation. Clearly, if a director is to avoid the risk of personal liability for wrongful trading he must be able to recognise the moment when the company can no longer avoid liquidation. He therefore needs to be aware of the company's current trading position and cash flow and confident that assets outweigh liabilities.

In order to implement the company's financial strategy the directors normally have control over the company's borrowings. The articles may place a limit on the amount the company can borrow without members' approval. If the directors exceed their borrowing powers the loan is generally valid unless the lender is aware of the irregularity, but the directors risk personal liability.

Directors usually also have responsibility for the company's dividend policy. Common practice is to give the board power to pay interim dividends and to declare a final dividend subject to members' approval. However, the precise rules laid down in the articles vary from company to company. In addition, there are statutory rules which require dividends to be paid only out of realised profits. Directors responsible for paying an illegal dividend may be personally liable to repay the company.

The issue of shares is one of the most complex areas in which directors are likely to become involved. In addition to the fiduciary duty to issue shares only for a proper purpose, there are many statutory restrictions. In particular, directors cannot issue shares without authority in the articles or from members, and in most cases must offer ordinary shares to existing shareholders on terms no worse than those on which they are being issued to others. There are also provisions in the Financial Services Act 1986 which effectively prevent a private company from offering its shares to the general public. Companies are entitled to purchase their own shares in certain circumstances, but there are strict rules to ensure that total share capital is maintained. Only private companies can purchase their own shares out of capital, and then only subject to strict safeguards for creditors.

The conduct of directors during take-overs and mergers is governed by the City Code on Take-overs and Mergers. Although this has no statutory force its authority is generally accepted in the City. Its principles require parties to a take-over or merger to act in good faith and to treat all shareholders fairly. Under the Companies Act members must generally approve any payments made to directors as part of take-over arrangements.

6.10 GENERAL

Directors must exercise their financial responsibilities in accordance with the principles of skill and care discussed in Chapter 3. This means that they must act with reasonable care and diligence and are entitled to place reasonable reliance on co-directors and officers of the company. In practical terms this is not always helpful advice and the courts have not attempted to improve on it by formulating precise rules.

However, *Palmer's Company Law* puts forward four specific responsibilities deduced from the decisions of the courts.

(a) Each director must ensure that the company's money is properly invested, unless delegation is authorised by the articles (*Re City Equitable Fire Insurance Co Ltd* [1925] Ch 407).

(b) Directors must be satisfied that the company's assets (in particular, stock, investments and fixed assets) are properly valued in the accounts. They should not rely on the chairman's assurance or an expression of belief by the auditors. If the individual director does not have the skill necessary to value such items he should insist on periodic independent valuations.

(c) A list of cheques to be authorised by the board should be presented at each board meeting (*Re City Equitable Fire Insurance Co Ltd* [1925] Ch 407).

(d) Directors must be satisfied that the company's securities are kept in a safe place.

These responsibilities are based on the specific circumstances of each case and should be regarded as guides to conduct rather than as hard and fast rules. For example, it is unlikely that under modern conditions the board would be able to authorise all payments. It is therefore important that directors implement proper controls over payments to ensure that cheques can only be issued by authorised personnel and when supported by documentation. The fundamental principle is that directors should act honestly and reasonably in the circumstances.

6.11 Borrowings

Before a company can legally borrow, it must have the power to do so. This is usually conferred by the memorandum, although trading companies have an implied power to borrow even without a specific clause to that effect.

It is the directors who normally exercise the company's power to borrow under their general authority to manage the business. However, the articles often make this power explicit with a clause enabling the directors to borrow money and mortgage the company's property and issue other security. It is quite common for the articles to limit the amount that the directors can borrow without shareholder approval, usually to a multiple of (say, two or three times) share capital and reserves. In Table A there is no such clause (although the previous version limited directors' power to borrow to the amount of share capital unless shareholder approval was obtained).

If the directors exceed their borrowing powers as permitted by the articles a lender is in the same position as any other party contracting with the company. Broadly, this means that the lending agreement is enforceable against the company unless the lender has actual notice that the borrowing limit is being exceeded (see paragraph 2.20 ff, above). Even if the lender has actual notice, the amendments made by the 1989 Act may make the agreement enforceable against the company (see paragraph 2.21, above). However, if a director exceeds his powers in borrowing on behalf of the company he may be personally liable for breach of implied warranty of authority.

6.20 SHARES

6.21 Issue of shares

The fiduciary rule which restricts directors from issuing shares except for a proper purpose is discussed in paragraph 3.22, above. In addition there is a series of statutory provisions in sections 80 to 116 which regulates the issue of share capital. These are somewhat complex and include various relaxations and exemptions which are not dealt with here. The following is a brief summary.

(a) The directors may not allot shares unless given authority by the articles or by ordinary resolution. Whatever the source of the authority, it can normally be conferred for no more than five years, but it may be renewed by the members in general meeting (section 80). A private company can elect to extend the authority for a fixed period beyond five years or for an indefinite period (section 80A). Such an election is made by elective resolution (see paragraph 7.30, below).

(b) Ordinary shares to be allotted for cash must first be offered pro rata to existing shareholders on terms similar to or more favourable than those on which they are to be issued to others (section 89). These pre-emption rights are designed to protect a shareholder from dilution of his shareholding as a result of a new share issue. Private companies can exclude pre-emption rights altogether by means of a provision in the memorandum or articles (section 91) and all companies can authorise the directors, normally for a maximum period of five years, to issue shares without regard to pre-emption rights (section 95).

(c) Shares may not under any circumstances be issued at a discount (section 100).

(d) A public company may not allot shares otherwise than for cash (except in connection with a take-over or merger) unless the consideration has been independently valued within the previous six months (section 103). The valuation report will usually be given by the auditor, who may rely on an expert valuation (section 108).

(e) A public company may not allot shares unless one-quarter of the nominal value and the whole of the share premium are paid up (section 101).

An allotment in breach of these rules is normally valid but may lead to the company and/or the directors incurring a liability. Also the allottee may be required to pay the company a further amount in respect of shares issued in contravention of (c), (d) and (e) above.

6.22 Redemption or purchase of own shares

A company may issue redeemable shares provided it meets the requirements laid down in the Act (sections 159 and 160).

(a) The articles must permit the issue of such shares.

(b) There must always be some non-redeemable shares in issue.

(c) The shares to be redeemed must be fully paid up.

(d) The shares must be redeemed out of distributable profits or out of the proceeds of an issue of new shares made for the purpose of the redemption (but see paragraph 6.23, below, regarding private companies). Any premium payable on redemption must be paid out of distributable profits unless the shares to be redeemed were originally issued at a premium. If so, the premium on redemption may be paid out of the proceeds of a fresh issue of shares made for the purpose, up to the lesser of the premium originally received on the shares to be redeemed, or the current balance on the share premium account (including any premium on the new shares).

(e) The shares must be cancelled on redemption. This does not reduce the authorised capital.

To the extent that the redemption or purchase of shares is not provided for by a new issue of shares, an amount equal to the nominal value of the shares acquired must be transferred to a capital redemption reserve. This reserve must be treated in all respects like share capital except that it may be used to issue bonus shares (section 170).

A company may purchase its own shares subject to these same basic conditions (section 162), but with the additional requirement of shareholders' approval.

For market purchases (that is, purchases of shares through The Stock Exchange (including the Unlisted Securities Market) a general authority conferred by ordinary resolution is sufficient, provided the following are specified:

(i) the maximum number of shares to be purchased;

(ii) the maximum and minimum price to be paid;

(iii) an expiry date for the authority (not later than 18 months after the resolution) (section 166).

For off-market purchases a special resolution approving the terms is required (section 164). For public companies this must include an expiry date which must be not later than 18 months after the resolution. The shares to be purchased or redeemed may not be counted in the voting on the special resolution.

6.23 Redemption or purchase out of capital

If authorised by its articles to do so, a private company may redeem or purchase its shares out of capital (section 171). The permissible capital payment is the acquisition price after deducting distributable profits and the proceeds of any new issue of shares. If the nominal value of the shares acquired is greater than the aggregate of the permissible capital payment and the proceeds of any new issue, the excess must be transferred to capital redemption reserve; if it is less, the difference may be written off share capital or any capital reserve.

The following safeguards must be met before a payment out of capital can lawfully be made (sections 173 to 175):

(a) the payment must be approved by a special resolution;

(b) the directors must make a statutory declaration (to be delivered to the registrar with a copy available at the meeting at which the resolution is passed and at the company's registered office for a specified period) specifying the amount of the 'permissible capital payment', and stating that, in their opinion, the company will be solvent after the payment and throughout the following year;

(c) a report by the company's auditors must be annexed to the directors' declaration confirming that the permissible capital payment has been properly calculated and that the directors' declaration is not unreasonable in all the circumstances;

(d) details of the proposed capital payment must be published in the Gazette and either in a national newspaper or in a written notice to each creditor. Creditors and members may apply to the court for the resolution to be cancelled. The payment must not be made less than five weeks or more than seven weeks after the date of the resolution.

If the company goes into insolvent liquidation within the period covered by the statutory declaration of solvency, the persons from whom the shares were bought are liable to repay the company to the extent necessary to remedy the deficiency (Insolvency Act 1986, section 76). The directors who signed the declaration are jointly and severally liable with those vendors unless they can show that they had reasonable grounds for the conclusion they formed as to the company's solvency.

6.24 Financial assistance for acquisition of own shares

Subject to certain exceptions, companies are generally prohibited from giving any kind of financial assistance related to the acquisition of their own or their holding company's shares (section 151). This prohibition does not apply where:

(a) the lending of money is part of the ordinary business of the company and the money is lent in the ordinary course of business; or

(b) the provision of financial assistance is made in good faith in the interests of the company, for the purposes of an employees' share scheme; or

(c) the provision of financial assistance is made to facilitate transactions between *bona fide* employees, ex-employees and certain connected persons in shares in the company or its holding company; or

(d) the loan is made to *bona fide* employees (not directors) to enable them to purchase shares in the company or its holding company to be held by them by way of beneficial ownership; or

(e) the principal purpose of the transaction is not to give financial assistance for the purpose of the acquisition of shares, or is incidental to some larger purpose, and the assistance is given in good faith in the interests of the company (section 153).

However, a public company may only give this financial assistance if its net assets are not thereby reduced or to the extent the net assets are reduced the assistance is provided out of distributable profits (section 154).

The prohibition does not apply to a private company which fulfils certain requirements for safeguarding the interests of shareholders and creditors (as set out in sections 156 and 157). The principal limitation is that any financial assistance must, to the extent that it reduces net assets, be made out of distributable profits. The safeguards include:

(a) approval by special resolution;

(b) a statutory declaration by the directors giving details of the arrangement, and stating that, in their opinion, the company will still be solvent after the arrangement and throughout the following year;

(c) a report by the auditors on the directors' statutory declaration;

(d) an application by not less than 10% of the members may be made to the courts for cancellation of the order.

Loans and other financial assistance which may be made by a company under the above rules must not include any loans etc to directors which are prohibited under section 330 (see Chapter 9).

If a company breaks the rules on giving financial assistance it is liable to a fine, and every officer in default is liable to imprisonment or a fine, or both (section 151).

6.25 Capital requirement of a public company

A public company must have a minimum authorised and issued share capital of £50,000 of which at least one-quarter, together with the whole of any share premium, is fully paid up (sections 117, 118). If the company reduces its share capital (which it may do either with the permission of the court or on the acquisition of its own shares) below £50,000, it must re-register as a private company (sections 139, 146).

If a public company's net assets fall to half or less of its called up share capital, the directors must convene an extraordinary general meeting. They have 28 days to do so from the day on which the fact first becomes known to one of their number, and the meeting must be within 56 days (section 142).

The Act does not dictate what action must be taken at the meeting, leaving the directors to make appropriate recommendations. However, trading while commercially insolvent may lead the courts to infer an intent to defraud, which is a criminal offence under section 458, and there are also penalties under the Insolvency Act (see Chapter 11).

6.30 DIVIDENDS

The articles normally give members the power to declare dividends in general meeting. In Table A, article 102 gives members the right to declare a dividend by ordinary resolution, so long as it does not exceed the amount recommended by the directors. However, the directors are authorised by article 103 to pay interim dividends which appear to be justified by the profits. If the articles do not make specific provision, the power to declare dividends lies with the directors under their general powers.

It is a fundamental rule of law that dividends may not be paid out of capital (*Re Exchange Banking Co, Flitcroft's Case* (1882) 21 Ch D 519). To do so is *ultra vires*. However, in case law there is, for example, no requirement to make good losses accumulated in prior years before paying a dividend out of current profits (*Ammonia Soda Co Ltd v Chamberlain* [1918] 1 Ch 266). This was reversed in 1980 when statutory provisions were introduced defining which profits are distributable and the circumstances in which they may legally be distributed. (These rules – sections 263 to 281 of the Act – are discussed in the following paragraphs.)

However, the Act specifically preserves any existing rules of law restricting dividends (section 281) and therefore is not necessarily enough merely to comply with the Act. For example, a dividend based on accounts which show available profits would be *ultra vires* if made after subsequent losses have eliminated the profits, although the requirements of the Act have ostensibly been met (see paragraph 6.34, below). Similarly, directors' common law duties (to act with reasonable skill and care in what they believe to be the best interests of the company) would generally preclude them from paying an imprudent dividend. Directors who make an unlawful dividend may be held personally liable to account for it to the company.

All the provisions of the Act regarding the payment of dividends and other distributions relate to individual companies only and not to groups.

6.31 Profits available for distribution

A distribution may only be made out of profits legally available for the purpose (section 263). A distribution does not include:

(a) an issue of fully or partly paid bonus shares;

(b) a redemption or purchase of a company's own shares out of capital (including the proceeds of any fresh issue of shares) or out of unrealised profits;

(c) certain reductions of capital;

(d) a distribution of assets in a winding up.

6.32 Payment of dividends

A private company can distribute the whole of its accumulated realised profits less its accumulated realised losses (section 263). It is not required to take account of unrealised losses. However, as indicated below a provision is usually to be treated as a realised loss.

A public company cannot distribute its realised profits without first making good any excess of unrealised losses over unrealised profits. It can make a distribution only if the distribution does not reduce the company's net assets below the aggregate of the called up share capital and undistributable reserves (section 264).

There are special rules for investment companies (sections 265 and 266) and insurance companies (section 268).

6.33 Realised profits and losses

Realised profits and losses are defined (in section 262 (3)) as profits or losses of the company as fall to be treated as realised in accordance with principles generally accepted, at the time when the accounts are prepared, with respect to the determination for accounting purposes of realised profits or losses. The joint accountancy bodies have issued guidance on realised and distributable profits which confirms that profits recognised in the profit and loss account in accordance with the Financial Reporting Standards issued by the Accounting Standards Board (see paragraph 5.36, above) should normally be treated as realised. In other circumstances profits will normally be treated as realised if they result from an accounting policy consistent with the accounting principles set out in the Act (Schedule 4, paragraphs 10 to 14, see paragraph 5.32, above). A surplus arising on the revaluation of an asset is not realised.

The prudence concept (see paragraph 5.32, above) is particularly important in determining whether an item is realised. Profits should not be anticipated and should only be recognised in the profit and loss account when realised either as cash or as assets the ultimate cash realisation of which can be assessed with reasonable certainty. Provision should be made for losses whether the amount is known or is merely an estimate.

In addition, the Act specifies how certain items are to be treated:

(a) Provisions for liabilities, charges, depreciation or diminution in the value of assets are realised losses (section 275). However, an exception is made for a fixed asset written down in value when all the assets (other than goodwill) are revalued. This useful exception is extended to circumstances where only certain assets (such as properties) have been revalued, provided the directors are satisfied that the other assets are worth at least their carrying value in the accounts.

(b) Excess depreciation (that is, the extent to which depreciation of a revalued asset exceeds the corresponding depreciation based on original cost) is a realised profit (section 275). Thus directors can increase distributable reserves by transferring the amount of excess depreciation from the revaluation reserve to the profit and loss account each year.

(c) Development costs carried forward as an asset are a realised loss unless the directors can come up with a good reason why not (section 269). Development costs are costs incurred prior to commercial production and should normally be written off unless they represent clearly defined expenditure on an identifiable project which is reasonably certain to succeed commercially (see Statement of Standard Accounting Practice No 13). If development costs meet these criteria the directors are justified in carrying them forward and not treating them as a realised loss.

(d) If a company makes a distribution in kind, any unrealised profit included in the carrying value of the non-cash asset distributed is regarded as realised (section 276). This provision is intended to assist demergers, in which real property or shares in group companies are sometimes transferred. However, it also applies to the distribution of a non-cash asset to an individual shareholder, which can be useful in private companies.

6.34 Relevant accounts

The amount of distributable profit is determined by reference to the 'relevant accounts'. These are normally the last annual accounts, but a company may produce interim accounts to show that further distributable profits are available (section 270). In the case of a public company the interim accounts must be prepared on the same basis as statutory annual accounts and delivered to the registrar, but they need not be audited (section 272).

If the company wants to make a distribution in respect of its first accounting period before accounts have been laid before members, it must prepare 'initial accounts' which, in the case of a public company, must be audited and filed (section 273).

If the auditors' report on the relevant accounts is qualified, before a distribution can be made on the basis of those accounts, the directors must obtain a statement from the auditors stating whether the qualification is material for deciding whether a distribution is lawful (sections 271 and 273).

6.40 PUBLIC ISSUES

The Financial Services Act 1986 replaced the old Companies Act rules dealing with public issues of shares and introduced an entirely new framework for controlling investment business as a whole. The detail of the Act is outside the scope of this book, but directors should be aware of some of the key provisions restricting the issue of securities.

6.41 Listed and unlisted securities

The Financial Services Act 1986 lays down separate rules for the admission of securities to the Official List of The Stock Exchange and for offers of unlisted securities. Only public companies can be admitted to the Official List (Financial Services Act 1986, section 143). A company applying for an Official Listing must furnish The Stock Exchange with the 'listing particulars' specified in the *Admission of Securities to Listing* (Yellow Book) (Financial Services Act 1986, section 144). The particulars must be published and filed with the registrar (Financial Services Act 1986, section 149).

References below are to Part V of the Financial Services Act 1986 which is due to replace Part III of the Companies Act 1985 in 1991 in relation to offers of unlisted securities.

Subject to certain exemptions public issues of unlisted securities require a prospectus, since a company cannot issue an advertisement offering its securities unless a prospectus in the prescribed form has been, or will be, filed with the registrar (Financial Services Act 1986, sections 159, 160).

An advertisement offers securities if it invites someone to enter into an agreement to acquire them, or contains information calculated to lead to someone entering into such an agreement (Financial Services Act 1986, section 158). Only a public company is allowed to issue an advertisement offering its securities (Financial Services Act 1986, section 170). A private company which contravenes this provision commits a criminal offence and cannot enforce any resulting agreement (Financial Services Act 1986, sections 171 and 57).

6.42 General duty of disclosure

Although the detailed requirements of the listing particulars are different from those of a prospectus, there are two principles in common:

(a) There must be all such information as a person would reasonably require for the purpose of making an informed assessment of the rights attaching to the securities and of the financial viability of the issuers (Financial Services Act 1986, sections 146 and 163).

(b) A person responsible for listing particulars or a prospectus is personally liable to pay compensation to anyone who acquires the securities and suffers loss as a result of an untrue or misleading statement, or omission (Financial Services Act 1986, sections 150 and 166), unless he has reasonable grounds for the statement (Financial Services Act 1986, sections 151 and 167).

In addition, directors may also be liable for damages for fraud under common law, or for negligent misstatement under the Misrepresentation Act 1967.

6.50 TAKE-OVERS AND MERGERS

Statutory provisions dealing with the conduct of take-overs and mergers are minimal. Broadly, such transactions are governed by the City Code on Take-overs and Mergers which has no legal force, as such, but is accepted by stockbrokers and merchant banks. In *Dunford & Elliott Ltd v Johnson & Firth Brown Ltd* [1977] 1 Lloyd's Rep 505 Lord Denning said, 'Although this Code does not have the force of law, nevertheless it does denote good business practice and good business standards'.

The Code is supervised by the Takeover Panel, which introduced a revised edition in October 1990. Further amendments are made from time to time. The Code consists of General Principles, augmented by detailed Rules, all of which must be followed in spirit as well as to precise wording. The underlying theme is that all participants should always act in good faith and treat all shareholders even-handedly.

The Stock Exchange rules for listed companies involved in a take-over bid require the offer document, which must include certain prescribed information, to be approved by the Quotations Department.

The major statutory provisions are in section 428 ff (as substituted by the Financial Services Act 1986, Schedule 12). In broad terms, a company which acquires 90% of a company has the right to purchase the remaining 10% on the same terms, subject to the minority's right to appeal to the court. In the same circumstances a minority shareholder may require the bidder to purchase his shares.

6.51 Payments to directors

To prevent directors feathering their own nests when their company is taken over, the Act makes provision for shareholders to approve any payment made to them.

(a) Under section 313, when all or part of the company's business or property is transferred, any payment made to a director in connection with his loss of office or retirement must be approved by members. Any payment made without approval is unlawful and deemed to be held in trust for the company.

(b) Under section 314, any payment to be made to a director in connection with his loss of office or retirement as a result of a take-over bid must be disclosed in the offer document. Shareholders thus have the opportunity to reject the bid if they object to the payment.

6.52 Fiduciary duty

The issue of shares by directors during a take-over has already been considered in paragraph 3.22, above. The *Bamford, Howard Smith* and *Hogg v Cramphorn* cases show that directors must issue shares for a proper purpose and cannot act purely out of self interest to reinforce their own position. But if they act honestly in the interests of the company their actions can be ratified by the company even if their self-interest is served.

7 Directors' relationship with shareholders

It is a fundamental principle of company law that the will of the company is determined by the majority of its members, subject to the provisions of the articles and the Act. The statutory provisions requiring certain acts of the company to be approved by resolution of the members in general meeting are obviously based on this principle. However, as we have seen, the will of the majority does not equate with majority rule. The members cannot normally manage the company by resolution in general meeting – or at least, not if Table A or other similar articles are adopted (see paragraph 2.14, above). However, they retain certain inalienable rights including the rights to dismiss a director and to change the articles by resolution in general meeting, and every company must hold an annual general meeting to allow shareholders to express their views unless, as a private company, the members have unanimously agreed to dispense with such a meeting (see paragraph 7.11, below).

General meetings, then, are an important feature of the company's machinery and one with which directors must have more than a nodding acquaintance. Apart from the annual general meeting, the directors are usually empowered to call an extraordinary general meeting for any reason, and can be compelled to do so by 10% of the members. Business cannot be transacted at a meeting unless a quorum – as laid down in the articles, but at least two members – is present. Voting at meetings is in the first instance by show of hands, but members generally have the right to demand a poll on the basis of one vote per share. Members have a statutory right to appoint proxies to vote for them at general meetings. An ordinary resolution requires only a simple majority of the votes actually cast, but a special resolution requires a 75% majority and a private companies elective resolution requires unanimous approval.

Private companies have been provided with a formal statutory alternative to holding meetings to pass resolutions. They are able to transact business by means of written resolutions (see paragraph 7.32, below).

In many private companies the directors are also the major shareholders. This combination of management control and voting power can put those members who are not directors at the mercy of the board. Directors who are major shareholders might, for example, be tempted to use the company's profits to pay themselves remuneration instead of declaring dividends. They might also try to use the company to further their other personal business interests rather than the interests of the company – voting in general meetings to ratify their alleged breaches of fiduciary duty (see paragraph 3.24, above).

The law is concerned to strike a balance between majority rule and unfair oppression of minorities. Minorities who suffer unjustly at the hands of directors can obtain a number of remedies through the courts, including the liquidation of the company.

7.10 GENERAL MEETINGS

7.11 Annual general meeting

An annual general meeting must be held each calendar year within 15 months of the last one (except for the first annual general meeting which must merely be held within 18 months of incorporation) (section 366). Only one AGM can be held in a calendar year. The duty to call an AGM lies with the directors and failure to do so leaves the company and every officer responsible liable to a default fine. If an AGM is not held, any member is entitled to apply to the Secretary of State, who has wide powers to call one. Private companies may elect to dispense with holding an AGM or to dispense with certain business normally dealt with at an AGM (see paragraph 7.30, below). Any member can require an AGM to be held when such an election is in force (section 366A).

Neither the Act nor Table A dictates what business must be carried out at an AGM. The agenda is therefore normally left to the directors, although the articles may specify that certain business must be transacted. A member may also propose a resolution.

The only business that Table A requires to be carried out specifically at the AGM is the election of directors retiring under the articles (for example, by rotation), but a number of other items are normally dealt with. The obvious example is the accounts, which are usually presented every year, and so may be conveniently dealt with at the AGM. However, the accounts are not a necessary part of the AGM and if, for example, a company extends its financial year in such a way that it has no financial year end in a particular calendar year it must still hold an AGM. There is no requirement for members to adopt or approve the accounts, which are therefore usually 'considered' or 'received' or sometimes both.

A number of items affecting the auditors are normally dealt with at an AGM at which accounts are received. Section 384 requires auditors to be appointed (or reappointed) at the same meeting except in the case of a private company which has elected to dispense with the laying of accounts or the obligation to appoint auditors annually. Section 390A provides for the remuneration of the auditors to be fixed either by the company in general meeting or in manner determined by the company in general meeting. The resolution put to the AGM usually gives the directors the power to fix the auditors' remuneration.

Other matters dealt with at the AGM usually include the declaration of a dividend (see paragraph 6.30, above) and sometimes, an authority for directors to issue shares (see paragraph 6.20 ff, above).

7.12 Extraordinary general meetings

The articles usually authorise the directors to call an extraordinary general meeting, and under Table A they may do so at any time, for any purpose (article 37). An extraordinary general meeting is any general meeting other than the AGM.

In addition, section 368 lays down one of the most important minority rights, by giving 10% of members (or holders of 10% of the issued share capital) the power to require the directors to call an extraordinary general meeting.

7.13 Class meetings

Class meetings are not general meetings but are confined to holders of a particular class of shares. Such meetings are required by the Act in certain circumstances, and in particular section 125 may require a meeting of the holders of a class of shares to sanction any variation in the rights attaching to those shares.

7.14 Notice of meetings

The length of notice required for convening an AGM is 21 days, unless a shorter period is unanimously agreed by members (section 369). Other meetings require 14 days' notice or 21 days if an elective resolution is to be moved (see paragraph 7.30, below). A shorter notice period is permissible provided 95% of members (or holders of 95% of the share capital) agree and the meeting is not considering an elective resolution (sections 369, 378 and 379A). Longer periods of notice may be specified by the articles.

There are no statutory requirements regarding the contents of the notice, except that the AGM must be described as such (section 366). The notice must therefore comply with the articles, and where Table A is adopted, article 38 requires the general nature of any business to be transacted at the AGM to be specified. This previously applied only to special business, but Table A no longer makes a distinction between special and ordinary business at an AGM. Where the articles do make such a distinction the directors must under common law give sufficient detail to enable a member to decide whether or not to attend. This requirement extends to any business to be transacted at an extraordinary general meeting.

Every notice calling a general meeting must state that a member entitled to attend and vote may appoint a proxy (section 372). In the case of listed companies, the notice must also state where and when the directors' service contracts can be inspected.

7.20 CONDUCT OF MEETINGS

Business cannot be transacted at a general meeting unless there is a quorum. This is defined in section 370 as 'two members personally present', unless the articles provide otherwise. One person cannot constitute a meeting (for example, *Re London Flats Ltd* [1969] 2 All ER 744) unless he is the holder of all the shares of a particular class at a class meeting (*East v Bennett Bros Ltd* [1911] 1 Ch 163) or the Secretary of State or the court so orders under sections 367 or 371.

A representative of a corporate shareholder counts towards a quorum and is entitled to exercise all the powers that the corporation has as a member (section 375).

Any member is entitled to appoint a proxy to attend the meeting and vote instead of him (section 372). The proxy is entitled to speak at the meeting of a private company, but may only do so in the case of a public company where the articles so provide. The Stock Exchange requires listed companies to send 'two-way' proxy forms to members (that is, forms which allow members to direct whether their votes should be cast for or against the resolution). This is not a requirement for other companies, although article 61 does provide for it.

Voting is in the first instance by show of hands, but article 46 allows the chairman or two members or holders of 10% of the voting rights to demand a poll. Section 373 provides that the articles cannot take away the right of at least five members, or holders of 10% of the voting capital, to demand a poll. In the absence of specific provision in the articles, common law allows any member to demand a poll.

The articles usually provide for a member to have one vote for every share he holds. However, the articles can specify a scale or any other arrangement (see, for example, *Bushell v Faith* [1970] AC 1099 in paragraph 1.42, above).

Minutes must be kept of general meetings and the minute book must be available for inspection (sections 382, 383).

7.21 The chairman

Under article 42 the chairman of the board takes the chair at general meetings. If he is absent or unwilling to act the directors may appoint one of their number and failing that members may elect any member as chairman. If there is no provision in the articles the members can elect the chairman (section 370).

The chairman's duties are:

(a) to keep order and to see that the company's business is properly conducted (*Re Indian Zoedone Co* (1884) 26 Ch D 70);

(b) to allow members a reasonable opportunity to speak, but to propose if he thinks fit that the discussion be terminated (*Wall v Exchange Investment Corpn* [1926] Ch 143);

(c) to ascertain the will of the meeting by show of hands or poll (the chairman has the right under article 46 to call for a poll);

(d) to decide incidental questions, such as the validity of proxies.

If Table A is adopted the chairman has a casting vote in the event of a tie on either a show of hands or a poll (article 50). He also has the right to adjourn meetings with the consent of the members or in the case of disorder.

7.30 RESOLUTIONS

There are four types of resolution under company law: ordinary, extraordinary, special and elective. Copies of all extraordinary, special and elective resolutions must be sent to the registrar, but only certain specified ordinary resolutions need be filed (section 380).

An ordinary resolution is passed if a simple majority of the valid votes actually cast at the meeting are in favour of it. An extraordinary resolution requires a 75% majority. A special resolution also requires a 75% majority but in addition members must have been given at least 21 days' notice of the intention to propose it as a special resolution. An elective resolution may only be passed by a private company and requires unanimous approval. Members must have been given at least 21 days' notice of the intention to propose it as an elective resolution.

Extraordinary resolutions are relatively rare, being used most frequently in a winding up, although they are also specified for the variation of certain class rights (section 125). Special resolutions, on the other hand, are very common since the Act specifies them as prerequisites for a number of important actions by the company. These include:

(a) alteration of objects (section 4);

(b) change of articles (section 9);

(c) change of name (section 28);

(d) re-registration as a public or private company (sections 43 and 53);

(e) re-registration as a limited company (section 51);

(f) disapplication of pre-emption rights (section 95);

(g) conversion of its uncalled share capital into reserve capital (that is, capital that can only be called up when the company is being wound up) (section 120);

(h) reduction of capital (section 135);

(i) provision of financial assistance by a private company for the purchase of its own shares (section 155);

(j) purchase of own shares (section 164);

(k) redemption or purchase of shares out of capital (section 173);

(l) non-appointment of an auditor by a dormant company (section 250).

Elective resolutions were introduced by the Companies Act 1989 and allow private companies to:

(a) dispense with holding an AGM (section 366A);

(b) dispense with laying accounts and reports before a general meeting (section 252);

(c) dispense with the annual reappointment of auditors (section 386);

(d) reduce the majority required to hold a general meeting at short notice (sections 369(4) and 378(3));

(e) allow directors to allot shares for an indefinite period (section 80A).

Certain ordinary resolutions require special notice (that is, 28 days' notice) to be given *to* the company (not by it) (section 379). These have been dealt with where they arise, and include resolutions:

(a) to remove a director;

(b) to appoint a director over the age of 70;

(c) to remove an auditor before his term has expired;

(d) to appoint an auditor other than the retiring auditor.

An ordinary resolution passed at a meeting does not have to be identical with the resolution proposed in the notice, so long as it is substantially the same. Extraordinary or special resolutions, however, are only valid if they follow the exact wording in the notice.

7.31 Informal resolutions

In the case of small private companies the formal requirements for passing resolutions are not always met, but the resolutions are still valid in certain circumstances.

(a) If all the members are present at a meeting and assent to a proposal it does not matter whether a formal resolution has been put (*Re Express Engineering Works Ltd* [1920] 1 Ch 466).

(b) Even if there is no meeting, the unanimous assent of members to a matter which is within the power of a general meeting will be as binding as a formal resolution (*Re Duomatic Ltd* [1969] 2 Ch 365 and *Parker & Cooper Ltd v Reading* [1926] Ch 975). This principle of unanimity applies also to special resolutions (*Cane v Jones* [1981] 1 All ER 533).

It hardly needs emphasising that wherever possible the formal procedures should be followed in order to avoid disputes.

7.32 Written resolutions

The Act allows to be done by written resolution anything that a private company can do by:

(a) resolution of the company in general meeting; or

(b) resolution of a meeting of any class of members of the company.

Written resolutions may not be used to remove a director or auditor from office before the expiry of the period of office (Schedule 15A, para 1).

No meeting needs to take place, nor is any notice required; however the resolution must be signed by all the members of the company who would have been entitled, at the date of the resolution, to attend and vote at the meeting (section 381A). Copies of written resolutions must be sent to the company's auditors who may require certain matters to go before a general meeting (section 381B). When passed the written resolution should be recorded in a book in the same way as the minutes of a general meeting are recorded (section 382A).

There are certain procedures to be followed for the following types of resolution:

(a) disapplication of pre-emption rights (Schedule 15A, para 3);

(b) financial assistance for purchase of company's own shares or those of holding company (Schedule 15A, para 4);

(c) authority for off-market purchase or contingent purchase contract of company's own shares (Schedule 15A, para 5);

(d) approval of payment out of capital (Schedule 15A, para 6);

(e) approval of director's service contract (Schedule 15A, para 7);

(f) funding of director's expenditure in performing duties (Schedule 15A, para 8).

7.40 PROTECTION OF MINORITIES

Where a minority of shareholders receives unfair treatment at the hands of the majority the law sometimes mitigates the general principle of majority rule. Unfortunately the common law provides little opportunity for the minority to defend itself, and (successive) statutes have not proved particularly effective. The following are possible avenues for redress:

(a) Rights under common law where there is fraud on the minority (see paragraph 7.42, below).

(b) Rights under section 368 to requisition an extraordinary general meeting (see paragraph 7.12, above).

(c) Rights under section 431 to apply to the Secretary of State to investigate the company's affairs (see paragraph 471, above).

(d) Right under section 122 of the Insolvency Act 1986 to apply for a just and equitable winding up (see paragraph 7.43, below).

(e) Right under section 459 to apply to the court for relief if the company's affairs are being conducted in a matter unfairly prejudicial to the minority or members generally (see paragraph 7.44, below).

7.41 Legal action by minorities

The general rule is that minority shareholders cannot sue for wrongs done to the company or for breaches of the company's own internal procedures, because the only proper plaintiff is the company itself as the wronged party. The leading case is *Foss v Harbottle* (1843) 2 Hare 461.

The implications of this ruling have persisted to the present day as a serious obstacle to the guarantee of fair treatment for minorities. Nevertheless, some exceptions to the rule in *Foss v Harbottle* have been developed. The following paragraph is, however, no more than a summary of a complex area.

7.42 Exceptions to the rule in *Foss v Harbottle*

The rule in *Foss v Harbottle* does not apply where the majority cannot ratify the company's action because:

(a) the act is illegal or, in certain circumstances, *ultra vires* (see paragraph 2.24, above);

(b) the resolution requires more than a simple majority;

(c) the act is a fraud on the minority and the wrongdoers control the company.

Of these, the first needs no explanation and the second must apply or a simple majority of members could continually override provisions requiring a 75% majority. However, the exception for a fraud on the minority is more complicated. Although the directors have a fiduciary duty to act *bona fide* in the best interests of the company as a whole and to exercise their powers for a proper purpose, breaches have sometimes been held to be ratifiable by the majority as, for example, in *Bamford v Bamford* (see paragraph 3.22, above) and

Regal (Hastings) v Gulliver (see paragraph 3.24, above). However, where the wrongdoers act fraudulently and use their control to prevent the company from bringing an action, the courts have allowed minority shareholders to do so.

In *Burland v Earle* [1902] AC 83, the minority sued, inter alia, to compel the directors to declare a dividend and to account to the company for personal profits made by selling assets to the company. The minority shareholders were allowed to bring an action in their own names 'in order to give a remedy for a wrong which would otherwise escape redress'. A similar judgement was given in *Menier v Hooper's Telegraph Works* (1874) 9 Ch App 350 where the majority shareholders were dealing with the assets of the company so as to benefit themselves at the expense of the minority. *Cook v Deeks* (see paragraph 3.24, above) also decided in favour of the minority.

7.43 Just and equitable winding up

An oppressed shareholder may apply to the court for the company to be wound up under section 122 of the Insolvency Act 1986. Orders have been made in a number of circumstances, of which the following variations on the same theme are important from the point of view of an oppressed minority:

(a) the company is in substance a partnership and there is deadlock or a complete breakdown of confidence which would justify the dissolution of a partnership (*Re Yenidje Tobacco Co Ltd* [1916] 2 Ch 426);

(b) an underlying obligation to allow the petitioner to participate in management has broken down (*Ebrahimi v Westbourne Galleries Ltd* [1973] AC 360) – see paragraph 1.42, above.

However, winding up is clearly a drastic solution to the problem of oppression, and section 459 provides a much more flexible remedy which is discussed in the following paragraph.

7.44 Statutory protection against unfair prejudice

Section 459 provides that any member may apply to the court for an order giving whatever relief the court thinks fit on the ground:

(a) that the company's affairs are being or have been conducted in a manner which is unfairly prejudicial to the interests of its members generally or of some part of the members including himself; or

(b) that any actual or proposed act or omission of the company is or would be so prejudicial.

This provision was introduced in the Companies Act 1980, and was therefore unavailable in the *Westbourne Galleries* case (see paragraph 1.42, above). Previously, section 210 of the Companies Act 1948 afforded a measure of relief to an oppressed minority, but in practice was invoked successfully in only two reported cases. Section 459 gives a much wider measure of relief. In particular:

(a) it is no longer necessary for the facts to be sufficient to justify a just and equitable winding up;

(b) the conduct does not have to meet the test of 'oppressive' which was interpreted to mean wrongful rather than merely unfair;

(c) an isolated act of oppression would have escaped under the old provisions but is now specifically included.

Section 459 was amended by the Companies Act 1989 so as to refer to the 'interests of its members generally'. This removes some doubt as to the scope of the section as identified in various cases (*Re a Company No 00370 of 1987* (1988) 4 BCC 506 and *Re Sam Weller & Sons Ltd* (*Re a Company No 00823A of 1987*) (1989) 5 BCC 810).

The court has a wide discretionary power to make any order it thinks fit when giving relief under section 459. This power includes (but is not limited to) the following (section 461):

(a) to regulate the conduct of the company's affairs;

(b) to require any action to be stopped or carried out;

(c) to authorise such persons as it directs to take civil proceedings in the company's name;

(d) to order the purchase of any member's shares by the company or other members.

The wide discretionary powers available to the court in giving relief have been confirmed by the Court of Appeal (*Re Bird Precision Bellows Ltd* [1985] 3 All ER 523). There is no overriding requirement that relief can be granted only if it is just and equitable and the petitioner is entirely blameless (*Re London School of Electronics Ltd* [1986] Ch 211). Further cases will have to be decided before a clearer understanding emerges of the availability and scope of the remedies under section 459. However, the rule in *Foss v Harbottle* has lost much of its power to restrict members from bringing actions against directors.

8 Directors' relationship with each other

The articles usually give the directors a large measure of freedom to call and conduct board meetings as they wish. Article 88 of Table A is fairly typical: 'Subject to the provisions of the articles, the directors may regulate their proceedings as they think fit'. Apart from the requirement to keep minutes there are no statutory rules at all, and, provided the collective agreement of the board can be established, it may not even be necessary for the directors to hold formal meetings. In practice, large companies tend to retain a degree of formality while small private companies often dispense with formal meetings almost entirely.

One advantage of more formal board meetings is that they provide a better framework for dealing with disagreements. Dissensions among board members is not unknown and it can be useful to have established procedures for airing opposing views and handling disputes. A director who finds himself in opposition to his boardroom colleagues must remember that his primary duty is to the company. On a purely commercial matter he can often best serve the company by accepting the majority decision and doing his best to implement it. However, where he believes a course of action is potentially damaging or illegal his duty requires more than silent acquiescence. He should at least ensure that his dissenting view is minuted, although that may not in itself be sufficient for him to escape liability. Resignation is the traditional alternative, but somewhat final, and if the company is insolvent the director cannot use it to escape his duty to creditors under the Insolvency Act.

The director may decide to remain in office in the hope of bringing about improvements or at least alerting members to the company's problems. However, a director who remains on the board in the face of clear mismanagement or malpractice must be able to point to positive steps he has taken if he is to escape liability. The court has power to exempt a director from liability if he has acted honestly and reasonably.

8.10 BOARD MEETINGS

A director has a general duty to attend board meetings when he reasonably can, but he need not attend all of them (*Re City Equitable Fire Insurance Co Ltd* [1925] Ch 407). Article 81 provides that a director loses office if he misses meetings for six consecutive months without permission of the board and the directors vote to remove him. Non-attendance can render a director liable for transactions of which he has no knowledge if his absence is held to be breach of duty, but otherwise he will not usually be liable for a decision taken in his absence unless he subsequently sanctions it or participates in its execution. Merely attending a board meeting at which minutes of a previous meeting are approved as correct will not make a director liable for something that took place while he was absent (*Re Lands Allotment Co* [1894] 1 Ch 616).

A director cannot lawfully be excluded from a board meeting and may obtain an injunction restraining further exclusion (*Pulbrook v Richmond Consolidated Mining Co* (1878) 9 Ch D 610).

Although former versions of Table A required directors to sign an attendance book at board meetings, there is no general requirement and the latest version omits it.

8.11 Notice

Under Table A, any director may call a meeting at any time and the secretary must do so at his request (article 88). The articles may provide for the form and length of notice, but if, as in Table A, there is no specific provision then reasonable notice must be given.

What is reasonable depends on the normal practice of the company. Thus in *Re Homer District Consolidated Gold Mines, ex p Smith* (1888) 39 Ch D 546 it was held that where notice was much shorter than normal and even reached one director after the meeting had taken place, the meeting was void. But while directors of a public company might expect written notice well in advance, directors of a private company can convene a valid board meeting on the spot if they all agree. A director who does not object to the short notice when he receives it is considered to have acquiesced to it and cannot subsequently claim a procedural defect had invalidated the meeting (*Browne v La Trinidad* (1887) 37 Ch D 1).

However, the fact that all the directors are physically present does not mean that a meeting can be convened against the wishes of a director. In *Barron v Potter* [1915] 3 KB 593 Potter met Barron at Paddington Station, and while walking alongside him on the platform formally proposed the election of three directors. Barron (according to Potter) replied, 'I object and I object to say anything to you at all.' Potter then used his casting vote as chairman to elect the three directors. The court held that the meeting was not a board meeting and that the elections were null and void.

In general it is necessary to give notice to all the directors, although article 88 makes an exception for any director who is abroad. It is not necessary to specify what business will be dealt with.

8.12 Quorum

Under article 89 the quorum for board meetings is two unless the directors set a different number. In the absence of provision in the articles a majority of the directors constitute a quorum unless the company's business is normally conducted by a different number (*York Tramways Co v Willows* (1882) 8 QBD 685). Since a private company may have only one director this can constitute a quorum.

Where a director has a material interest in a matter before the board which may conflict with the interests of the company he is not allowed to vote on it (article 94). Furthermore, he does not count towards a quorum (article 95). It is therefore possible that the meeting will become inquorate when it addresses a particular piece of business. When this happens the remaining directors can act only to fill vacancies or to call a general meeting (article 90). However, the general meeting can by ordinary resolution amend or remove any prohibition in the articles on directors voting at a board meeting: article 96 specifies that this can be achieved by ordinary resolution although normally the articles can only be overridden by special resolution.

8.13 Conduct of meetings

Article 91 allows the directors to appoint a chairman to preside over board meetings. If there is no chairman, or if he has not arrived within five minutes of the scheduled start, or if he is unwilling to act, the directors may elect someone else.

Questions arising at a board meeting are normally decided by a simple majority, with the chairman having a casting vote (article 88). The chairman's casting vote does not arise under common law and to have effect must be specified in the articles. It is, of course, always open to the articles to specify different voting rights or procedures.

Under article 93, a resolution signed by all the directors has the same validity as if it had been passed at a meeting. In the case of a one-member board it is advisable for the director to act always by means of written resolution, so as to avoid the eventuality of having to prove he held a meeting with himself.

8.14 Minutes

Section 382 requires minutes to be kept of all general meetings, directors' meetings and meetings of managers. This is reinforced by article 100 which specifies that there must be a record of all appointments of officers and of the proceedings at all members' and directors' meetings. The duty to keep minutes is usually delegated to the secretary.

Minutes are intended to be a record of decisions taken, with a short narrative whenever an explanation is considered necessary. It is not usual to record dissenting views unless the dissenting director specifically requests it.

Under section 382 minutes signed by the chairman are evidence – but not conclusive evidence – of the proceedings. The courts will admit alternative evidence to show that they are incomplete or inaccurate. It was held in *Re Fireproof Doors Ltd* [1916] 2 Ch 142 that decisions not recorded in the minutes may be proved by alternative evidence.

It is not legally necessary for minutes to be confirmed or adopted, and the chairman has the right to sign them without reference to the board. However, it is almost universal practice for the minutes to be submitted to the board for approval. Note that approval extends only to the accuracy of the minutes as a record of what was decided and not to the decisions themselves.

Members have no right to inspect the minutes of directors' meetings. Directors have a common law right to do so (*McCusker v McRae* 1966 SC 253). The auditors' statutory right of access to the company's books (section 237) includes board minutes.

8.20 DISAGREEMENT AMONG DIRECTORS

Where a director believes a course of action decided on by the board is either potentially damaging or improper, his duty to the company extends beyond an adverse vote.

(a) *Formal objection* As a minimum, the director should ensure that his opposition is minuted, but this does not necessarily free him from liability. It is open to him (under Table A) to call a board meeting and circulate his views to fellow directors beforehand. Unfortunately there is no compulsion for other directors to attend such a meeting; and if the full board has already considered the matter there will usually be no reason to suppose that it will reach a different conclusion.

(b) *Resignation* In some cases the director may feel that resignation is the best option available, particularly if he wants to avoid personal responsibility for the activities of the board. The threat of resignation is a valuable weapon in itself, but with the drawback that it can only be discharged once. In addition, if the company is insolvent resignation is unlikely to be regarded as a proper fulfilment of the duty under the Insolvency Act 1986 to minimise the potential loss to creditors (see Chapter 11).

(c) *Appeal to the members* Remembering that he has a primary duty to the company, the director may feel obliged to remain in office in order to be better placed to bring about improvements. Unless the articles provide for dismissal by the board any attempt to dismiss a dissenting director must be dealt with by the members in general meeting, which will give him the opportunity to circulate details of the dispute to members (see paragraph 1.42, above). If he cannot tempt the board to try to dismiss him through the medium of a general meeting, he may be able to mobilise enough support to requisition an extraordinary general meeting himself (or indeed, he may personally control the requisite 10% of voting capital). It is worth bearing in mind that a director who remains in office is in a stronger position to put his views to members, since the board will find it more difficult to prevent him publicising confidential information gained by virtue of his office. It is not, of course, usually open to the members to dictate to the directors (see paragraph 2.12, above). On the other hand, it is not easy for directors to act persistently against the wishes of the majority of members.

The dissenting director also has three other courses of action already considered which may be available in certain circumstances.

(a) Application for a court order under section 459 where the company's affairs have been conducted in a manner unfairly prejudicial to the interests of its members generally or to a minority of members. This application must be made by a member (see paragraph 7.44, above).

(b) Application to the Secretary of State for an investigation into the company's affairs. This application must be supported by a prescribed minimum of members (see paragraph 4.71, above).

(c) Application to the court for a just and equitable winding up (see paragraph 7.43, above).

9 Remuneration

9.10 The articles

9.11 Fees of trustee and nominee directors
9.12 Expenses
9.13 Tax-free payments prohibited

9.20 Service contracts

9.30 Claims for unpaid remuneration

9.31 Claims in insolvency

9.40 Compensation for loss of office

9.50 Disclosure in the accounts

A director has no right under common law to be paid for his services (Hutton v West Cork Rly Co (*1883*) *23 Ch D 654*). *However, this rather Victorian assumption that directors donate their services for nothing is usually overcome by a provision in the articles.*

Remuneration as a director is distinct from remuneration as an employee. Broadly speaking it is easier for a director – in the event of a dispute or the liquidation of the company – to enforce payment of salary for employment rather than director's fees. A director is only an employee of the company if he has a contract to that effect, and even directors who carry out executive functions are unlikely to have the rights of employees unless they have such a contract.

The accounts must disclose the total remuneration of everyone who was a director at any time during the financial year. The disclosure must distinguish between emoluments, pensions (excluding those substantially funded by contributions), compensation for loss of office and payments to third parties. If the company is a member of a group or aggregate remuneration exceeds £60,000, the notes must also disclose the chairman's emoluments, the emoluments of the highest-paid director (if not the chairman) and the number of directors whose emoluments fall within successive bands of £5,000. The legislation is widely drawn to include disclosure of all amounts payable to a director in respect of his duties as a director or executive, irrespective of who actually makes or receives the payment and whether they are paid in cash or in some other form.

9.10 THE ARTICLES

Directors have no right to remuneration unless the articles provide for it. Article 82 of Table A entitles directors to such remuneration as is voted to them by ordinary resolution. This is not entirely satisfactory for many companies, and a special article allowing the directors to fix their own remuneration is commonly adopted.

Article 82 also provides that directors' remuneration 'shall be deemed to accrue from day to day' so that a director who serves for part of a year is entitled to a proportion of his annual remuneration. In the absence of such a provision a fee of so much per annum may imply that a full year must be served before any remuneration can be claimed.

9.11 Fees of trustee and nominee directors

Trustees are often appointed to the board of a company by virtue of the trust's holding in it. The common law rule is that a trustee must not profit from his trust. However, if the will or deed of settlement clearly provides for the trustee to retain director's fees he is entitled to do so.

A nominee director is usually entitled to retain director's fees, since they arise from his contract of service with the company for which he is acting, and the nominating company has agreed to the contract by nominating him. In *Re Dover Coalfield Extension Ltd* [1908] 1 Ch 65 a director held qualification shares as nominee, but was allowed to retain his remuneration because it arose from his duties as a director, not because of his shareholding.

In summary, the trustee or nominee director should ensure that there is a clear authority for him to retain director's fees.

9.12 Expenses

Unless the articles provide for directors to be reimbursed for travelling and accommodation expenses connected with board meetings they are not entitled to claim them. However, article 83 includes such a provision, and includes all other expenses properly incurred by the directors in connection with the discharge of their duties. (See also paragraph 10.25, below.)

9.13 Tax-free payments prohibited

Tax-free payments to directors are prohibited by section 311, which provides that any agreement to pay a sum net of tax has the effect only of making the net amount a gross sum subject to income tax. The section is widely drawn to include any remuneration calculated by reference to or varying with the amount or rate of income tax.

9.20 SERVICE CONTRACTS

There is an important distinction between the director's separate roles as director and employee (see also paragraph 1.14, above). Whether a director is also an employee is a matter of fact, evidenced by a contract of employment. Under the Employment Protection (Consolidation) Act 1978 the main terms of employment of all employees must be put in writing even if there is no formal contract of employment.

In practice, directors who carry out executive functions are well advised to ensure that they have a written contract, since the courts are reluctant to hold that one exists based merely on the conduct of the parties. In *Parsons v Albert J Parsons & Sons Ltd* [1979] ICR 271 the court held that in the absence of a written or oral contract a director who worked full-time in the business was nevertheless not an employee.

The *Parsons* case also highlights the distinction usually drawn between fees – paid in respect of non-executive services as a director – and salaries – paid in respect of executive services as an employee. In this case the court noted that the director's remuneration was described in the accounts as 'fees'.

The Institute of Directors has a specimen form of service contract which includes most of the common provisions. The director must usually devote the whole of his attention to the company, refrain from competing with the company (except for minority holdings in listed companies) and keep details of the company's business confidential. The contract should also deal with executive duties, pay, holidays, sickness, pension, notice and dismissal procedures, among other things.

Under section 319 a director's service contract cannot provide for a period of employment exceeding five years unless the members in general meeting approve. Employment includes consultancy contracts. This prevents directors awarding themselves long service contracts as protection against dismissal by members under section 303.

9.30 CLAIMS FOR UNPAID REMUNERATION

The question of whether the director is being paid as a director or as an employee has an important bearing on whether he can claim the money in the event of non-payment. It is well established that a mere provision in the articles to remunerate directors does not itself give a director grounds for action (for example, *Hickman v Kent or*

Romney Marsh Sheep-Breeders Association [1915] 1 Ch 881). However, in the absence of specific terms in a service contract it may be possible to incorporate provisions of the articles in an implied contract if these were the grounds on which the director accepted office.

Thus a provision in the articles to pay a director implies acceptance by the company that it will pay for services rendered. In *Craven-Ellis v Canons Ltd* [1936] 2 KB 403 it was held that a managing director whose appointment was faulty was still entitled to a reasonable sum (*quantum meruit*) in respect of work actually performed.

On the other hand, where there is an express contract providing for remuneration to be fixed by the board or the members, a director cannot sue for *quantum meruit* unless the appropriate resolution has been passed. In *Re Richmond Gate Property Co Ltd* [1964] 3 All ER 936 the articles allowed the managing director to be paid such remuneration 'as the directors may determine'. The company went into liquidation before the directors had decided on remuneration, and the managing director was unable to claim.

It has to be said that the cases in this area are not entirely conclusive, and it is vital for a director to have a service contract which is specific on the subject of remuneration. It also seems that the courts require a strict adherence to the formalities when directors are remunerating themselves. In *Re J Franklin & Son Ltd* [1937] 4 All ER 43 it was held that remuneration voted to the directors at a general meeting which was inquorate (although only technically so) had to be repaid to the company.

9.31 Claims in insolvency

In the event of the company going into liquidation, properly authorised remuneration ranks as an unsecured debt in most cases. However, four months' wages or salary due to an employee ranks as a preferred debt (Insolvency Act 1986, Schedule 6, paragraph 9). It may be that a director who is also an employee could treat arrears of salary payable in respect of his employee functions as such a debt (for example, *Re Beeton & Co Ltd* [1913] 2 Ch 279).

9.40 COMPENSATION FOR LOSS OF OFFICE

As we have seen, a director can always be removed by the members under section 303, and possibly by the board if the articles allow (paragraph 1.43, above). Particulars of compensation paid to a director in respect of his dismissal or retirement must be disclosed to the members and approved by them (section 312). However, a payment of damages for breach of contract is not treated as compensation for this purpose (section 316) and nor is a payment made under a provision in the director's contract (*Taupo Totara Timber Co Ltd v Rowe* [1978] AC 537).

The distinction already made between the director's separate roles as director and employee (paragraph 1.14, above) is equally important when considering his entitlement to compensation for loss of office. An executive director has statutory rights as an employee under the Employment Protection (Consolidation) Act 1978. These relate principally to minimum periods of notice, redundancy payments and unfair dismissal.

If the director is not an employee his service contract may still give him the right to compensation. For example, if his contract specifies term of office or period of notice, premature removal will entitle him to damages. On the other hand, where there is no such provision, the general right of the company to remove him means that he has no claim for compensation.

9.50 DISCLOSURE IN THE ACCOUNTS

The notes to the accounts must disclose separately the aggregate amounts of directors' emoluments, directors' and past directors' pensions, any compensation paid to directors or past directors in respect of loss of office and amounts paid to an unconnected third party for making available the services of a person who has acted as director (section 232 and Schedule 6, paragraphs 1–14). In each case a distinction must be made between amounts paid in respect of services as a director and other amounts. This usually leads to emoluments being split between fees and salaries, but the directors may make any apportionment they think appropriate. If any director waives rights to emoluments, the number of directors doing so and the aggregate amounts waived must be disclosed. In the case of compensation for loss of office, a further distinction must be made between sums paid by the company, by its subsidiaries and by anyone else.

Amounts paid to a director include amounts paid to or receivable by a person connected with him or a body corporate controlled by him (Schedule 6, paragraph 10).

The following points should be noted:

(a) group accounts should only disclose payments to directors of the parent company;

(b) the disclosable amount includes all relevant payments by the company, its subsidiaries or any other person;

(c) emoluments include pension contributions paid on a director's behalf and the money value of any benefits in kind;

(d) all amounts receivable by a director in respect of the financial year must be included, even if paid after the year end: for example, a bonus based on profits or fees which can only be paid after approval at the AGM;

(e) the amount disclosed in respect of pensions should not include payments from a funded pension scheme;

(f) where the aggregate amounts paid in respect of directors' pensions, compensation for loss of office or paid to unconnected third parties include benefits other than in cash; the nature of such benefits must be disclosed.

Any transfer of a non-cash asset will be subject to the provisions relating to substantial property transactions (see paragraph 4.20, above).

Where the aggregate of emoluments exceeds £60,000 or the company is a member of a group a note to the accounts must show:

(a) the chairman's emoluments;

(b) the emoluments of the highest paid director (if not the chairman);

(c) the number of directors whose emoluments did not exceed £5,000;

(d) the number of directors whose emoluments were in each successive band of £5,000.

Emoluments for these purposes exclude pension contributions. Directors who performed their duties wholly or mainly outside the UK are ignored.

Directors have a duty to disclose to the company any amounts which fall to be disclosed under any of these provisions (section 232).

10 Loans to directors

There are extensive and complex statutory rules to prevent directors – including shadow directors – from abusing their position by borrowing money from the company. These rules operate within the wider fiduciary framework which prohibits a director from making a personal profit from his position in the company and which requires him to make the best use he can of its assets.

In essence a company must not lend more than £5,000 to a director or to a director of its holding company. If it does so the director is liable to repay the loan and make good any resultant loss. In addition, if the company is a public company (or there is a public company in the same group), anyone involved is guilty of a criminal offence.

The ban extends to certain indirect arrangements – including any arrangements with persons connected with a director – which might otherwise be used to evade the law. A wider range of transactions is prohibited if a public company is involved. On the other hand, there are a number of statutory exceptions to allow innocuous transactions to take place unhindered.

The annual accounts must disclose details of loans to, and other arrangements with, directors (whether or not they are illegal), as well as any contract with the company in which a director has a material interest.

There are special rules for banks and other companies which lend money in the normal course of their business.

All the rules in this area are particularly complex and consequently professional advice should be sought in any case of doubt.

10.10 GENERAL RESTRICTION

Section 330 prohibits a company from making loans to its directors or from guaranteeing loans to them by third parties. The ban applies to directors both of the company and of its holding company, but loans by a holding company to a director of its subsidiary are permitted. Shadow directors are treated as directors for the purposes of all the rules on loans.

In the case of relevant companies, the basic prohibition is extended to include:

(a) loans to connected persons;

(b) quasi-loans to directors or persons connected with them;

(c) credit transactions involving directors or connected persons;

(d) the provision of any guarantee or security in connection with a loan, quasi-loan or credit transaction made by any other person for a director or connected person.

10.11 Definitions

The Act does not define a loan, but in *Champagne Perrier-Jouet SA v H H Finch Ltd* [1982] 3 All ER 713 it was held that the correct meaning of loan was 'a sum of money lent for a time to be returned in money or money's worth'. Thus an essential ingredient of a loan is that the parties intend it to be repaid at some future time. Money which is not to be repaid will usually be treated as remuneration.

The legislation introduces four concepts which are important to an understanding of the rules (sections 331 and 346):

Relevant company A public company or a member of a group containing a public company.

Quasi-loan An arrangement under which the company pays an amount on behalf of the director on the understanding that it will be reimbursed. An example is when a director uses a company credit card for personal expenditure and reimburses the company.

Credit transaction Where the company sells anything to a director on any terms involving deferred payment, including leases, hire-purchase transactions and conditional sale agreements.

Connected person Persons connected with a director are, broadly, spouse and minor children, associated companies (ie those in which the director has a 20% or greater interest), trustees of family trusts, and business partners. The definition is given in section 346 and is too complex – particularly in relation to associated companies – to be given here in detail. However, it is worth noting that parents, brothers and sisters and adult offspring are not connected although in some cases transactions with them may be disclosable (see paragraph 10.52, below).

10.12 Indirect arrangements

Section 330 includes two additional rules prohibiting all companies from indirect arrangements which might otherwise be used to avoid the general ban.

(a) A company cannot take over any rights or obligations under a transaction which the Act prevents it from entering into directly. Thus the company cannot purchase the right to repayment of a loan made originally by a third party.

(b) A company cannot take part in an arrangement under which somebody else enters into a transaction which would be barred to the company under the Act, and the other person obtains some benefit from the company (or another group company). This catches, in particular, back-to-back loans by the company to directors of another company in return for loans to its own directors. The term 'arrangement' is deliberately wide: it is not restricted to a contractually binding agreement and may involve several parties and transactions.

10.20 PERMITTED TRANSACTIONS

The Act sets out a number of exceptions to the restrictions outlined above. However, most of these permitted transactions are nevertheless disclosable.

It is worth bearing in mind that the statutory rules are in a sense only a minimum. The company's memorandum or articles may be more restrictive than the Act; and similarly, the director should always be aware that the Act is no more than a specific statement of a fiduciary duty, which in a general way may impose wider restrictions.

10.21 Loans not exceeding £5,000

Any company may make loans of up to £5,000 to a director or a director of its holding company (section 334). This exception does not allow a relevant company to make a quasi-loan or a loan to a connected person, and does not extend to guarantees of loans. The Act does not set a maximum repayment period.

10.22 Short-term quasi-loans

A relevant company may make quasi-loans of up to £5,000 to a director or to a director of its holding company, provided the company is to be reimbursed within two months (section 332). This exception does not extend to quasi-loans to connected persons or to guarantees of quasi-loans.

10.23 Minor credit transactions and business transactions

A relevant company may make quasi-loans of up to £5,000 to a director or to a director of its holding company, provided the up to a limit of £10,000. If the transaction is entered into on arm's length terms in the ordinary course of business there is no upper limit (section 335).

10.24 Intra-group transactions

A company is not prohibited from making a loan, quasi-loan, credit transaction or any similar facility to its holding company (section 336).

A relevant company may make or guarantee a loan or quasi-loan to another member of its group, even if the receiving company is regarded as a person connected with a director of the lending company by virtue of being associated with him (section 333).

10.25 Directors' expenses

Any company may provide its own directors with funds to meet expenses incurred for the purposes of the company or in performance of their duties (section 337). The loan must have been given prior approval at a general meeting, or made on condition that if it is not approved at the next AGM it will be repaid within six months of it. A relevant company must not lend more than £20,000 to a director under this exception.

It is worth bearing in mind that this statutory exception is intended to cover circumstances in which the director is to repay the company. A common example would be a bridging loan to a director required by the company to move house for business purposes. Advances to directors to meet expenses to be incurred on the company's business are not prohibited by the Act because there is no question of reimbursement, and so there is no provision of credit. However, every case must be considered on its merits and with regard to the substance of the transaction. For example, money advanced to a director on account of remuneration (for example, a bonus which only becomes payable when approved at the annual general meeting) is not a loan. However, if Pay As You Earn is not deducted as required by section 311, then the payment may assume the characteristics of a loan. Similarly, any advance which is clearly in excess of the business expenses which a director could reasonably be expected to incur within a reasonable time could be interpreted as an attempt to give the director personal use of the money, and so be treated as a loan.

10.30 RECOGNISED BANKS AND OTHER MONEY-LENDING COMPANIES

The Act allows banking companies to make unlimited loans and quasi-loans to directors on their normal commercial terms (section 338). They may also lend up to £100,000 to each director as a subsidised home loan. Other money-lending companies have similar exemptions unless they are relevant companies. If so they may only lend up to a total permissible amount of £100,000 per director whether as a normal commercial loan or as a subsidised home loan. These rules are summarised in Appendix IV.

A money-lending company is a company whose normal business includes giving loans or quasi-loans or related guarantees. A banking company is a company authorised under the Banking Act 1987.

10.40 PENALTIES FOR CONTRAVENTION

The company is entitled to recover money or other property held by a director as the result of a prohibited transaction or arrangement unless:

(a) restitution is no longer possible;

(b) the company has been otherwise indemnified; or

(c) it would affect rights acquired for value by an innocent third party.

The director is liable to pay to the company any direct or indirect profit he has made from the prohibited transaction and to make good to the company any resultant loss or damage it has suffered (section 341).

In addition, it is a criminal offence for a relevant company to enter into a prohibited transaction or arrangement (section 342). However, it is a defence for the company that it did not know the relevant circumstances at the time of entering into the transaction. A director who, with reasonable cause to believe it is a contravention of section 330, permits or authorises the transaction is liable to a fine and up to two years imprisonment. Anyone else who procures the transaction is also criminally liable.

10.50 DISCLOSURE OF LOANS AND MATERIAL INTERESTS IN CONTRACTS

10.51 Requirement to disclose

The Act requires the annual accounts to contain details of loans and similar transactions involving directors (including shadow directors) and persons connected with them (section 232). The requirement applies to any transaction or arrangement described in section 330, including loans, quasi-loans, credit transactions and guarantees or provisions of security for any of these transactions (Schedule 6, paragraphs 15–17).

The disclosure requirement is extended to include also any other transaction or arrangement in which a director has a material interest (see paragraph 10.52, below).

Disclosure is specifically required whether or not (Schedule 6, paragraph 19):

(a) the transaction or arrangement is prohibited under the Act;

(b) the person for whom it was made was a director or connected person at the time it was made; or

(c) the subsidiary making the transaction was a subsidiary at the time it was made.

If the company fails to make the requisite disclosure, the auditors must do so in their report (section 237).

10.52 Disclosure of material interests in contracts

Section 317 requires a director (including a shadow director) to disclose to the board the nature of any direct or indirect interest he or a connected person has in any transaction or arrangement with the company. For this purpose the transaction or arrangement does not have to constitute a legal contract. This requirement cannot be waived by the articles.

As far as the accounts are concerned, only those contracts in which the director has a material interest need to be disclosed. Materiality is judged by the other members of the board, but the Act gives no guidance on how they should arrive at a conclusion. Perhaps the best approach is to consider whether knowledge of the interest is likely to be significant to users of the accounts. On this basis, it would not be necessary to disclose a director's interest in an insignificant transaction merely because the interest is material to the transaction; on the other hand an item should not escape disclosure on the ground that the amount is small in relation to the amounts in the accounts.

The Act specifically provides that if a majority of the directors resolves that an interest is not material, then that is conclusive (Schedule 6, paragraph 17).

10.53 Particulars to be disclosed

The accounts must disclose the following particulars (Schedule 6, paragraph 22):

(a) the principal terms of the transaction;

(b) a statement that the loan, guarantee, transaction etc was made or subsisted during the financial year;

(c) the name of the person for whom it was made (if the person is a connected person, the name of the director with whom he is connected must also be given);

(d) in the case of a loan made or to be made, the amount of the liability in respect of principal and interest at the beginning and end of the financial year, the maximum amount of the liability during the financial year, any interest due which has not been paid, and the amount of any provision made against the loan or accrued interest;

(e) where a company has guaranteed, or provided security for a loan, the amount for which the company was liable at the beginning and end of the financial year, the maximum potential liability, and the amount of any actual liability incurred;

(f) in the case of quasi-loans and credit transactions, the value of the transaction;

(g) in the case of any other transaction or arrangement in which a director had a material interest, the name of the director concerned and the nature of the interest, and the value of the transaction or arrangement.

The value of a transaction or arrangement is the value which would be attached on an arm's length basis in the ordinary course of business to the goods or services which are the subject of the transaction. If the transaction is a loan or guarantee it is the principal of the loan or the amount guaranteed or secured (section 340).

10.54 Exemptions from disclosure

The accounts do not need to disclose particulars of (Schedule 6):

(a) contracts between one company and another in which a director is interested only by virtue of being a director of the other company (paragraph 18);

(b) directors' service contracts (but contracts for services, such as consultancy contracts, must be disclosed) (paragraph 18);

(c) 'material interest' transactions which:

  (i) are entered into by the company in the ordinary course of business and on an arm's length basis (paragraph 20); or

  (ii) do not exceed £1,000 in aggregate for each director or if they do exceed £1,000 do not exceed the lower of £5,000 or 1% of the net assets of the company at the year end (paragraph 25);

(d) credit transactions (and related arrangements) which do not exceed £5,000 in aggregate for each director (paragraph 24).

11 Duties and liabilities of directors in respect of insolvent companies

The previous chapters of this book assume that the company is a going concern and that the directors are carrying out their duties without the threat of impending insolvency. However, the Insolvency Act 1986 contains provisions which are designed to curb improper activities by directors in the period leading up to a liquidation and which affect their day-to-day responsibilities. The provisions are enforced by making directors personally liable to compensate the company or creditors if they:

— *involve themselves in the management of a company while disqualified (see Chapter 1);*

— *misappropriate the company's funds or otherwise breach their duty to it;*

— *are guilty of fraudulent or wrongful trading;*

— *break the rules on re-using the names of insolvent companies.*

Fraudulent trading is also a criminal offence under the Companies Act. Wrongful trading is a concept originally introduced in the Insolvency Act 1985 to describe circumstances in which a director knows – or ought to know – that his company cannot avoid insolvent liquidation, and does not take every step he ought to take to minimise any potential loss to creditors.

11.10 THE INSOLVENCY ACTS 1985 AND 1986

The Insolvency Act 1985 introduced a new legal framework for the regulation of corporate and individual insolvencies. Because of its far-reaching effect on the provisions of the Companies Act 1985 relating to the appointment of receivers and the winding up of companies, the various strands of the legislation were consolidated into a single Insolvency Act 1986.

Although most of the 1986 Act is concerned with detailed technical provisions relating to the regulation and conduct of insolvencies, there are other provisions relating to the management of companies prior to insolvency which have a direct impact on directors. Most importantly, the Insolvency Act 1986 reinforces the duty of directors to creditors by means of the wrongful trading provisions.

11.11 Administrator

The Insolvency Act 1985 introduced a procedure for the appointment of an administrator to take charge of the company's affairs on behalf of all its creditors as a means of averting liquidation. The administrator is appointed by the court with the power to remove or appoint directors and authority to manage the company subject to the control of the court.

11.12 Administrative receiver

An administrative receiver is a receiver or manager of the whole (or substantially the whole) of a company's property, appointed by the holders of a debenture of the company secured by a floating charge.

11.13 Office holder

The Insolvency Act 1986 uses the term 'office holder' as a generic title for an insolvency practitioner acting in relation to a company, whether in the capacity of liquidator, administrator or administrative receiver, and the term has been used where appropriate in the following paragraphs. A liquidation and a winding up are the same thing.

Directors, other officers and anyone who has been an employee of the company within a year of the office holder taking office have a duty to co-operate with the office holder (Insolvency Act 1986, section 235). They must provide any information required and attend on the office holder in response to a reasonable requirement. Failure to comply with this provision is a criminal offence.

11.14 Definition of insolvency

The Insolvency Act 1985 expanded on the previous definition of insolvency contained in the Companies Act 1985 by deeming that a company is insolvent not only if it is unable to pay its debts as they fall due but also if the value of its assets is less than that of its liabilities, including contingent and prospective liabilities (Insolvency Act 1986, section 123).

There are obvious difficulties in arriving at the values required for this so-called 'asset test'. Balance sheet figures may be inappropriate and there is no guidance on how contingent and prospective liabilities should be taken into account. The extent to which this imposes an additional responsibility on directors will only be clarified as legal cases are decided.

11.20 PERSONAL LIABILITY OF DIRECTORS

Directors may incur personal liability to contribute to the company's assets in a winding up in the following ways:

(a) for misfeasance or breach of duty (Insolvency Act 1986, section 212, see paragraph 11.21, below);

(b) for fraudulent trading (Insolvency Act 1986, section 213, see paragraph 11.22, below);

(c) for wrongful trading (Insolvency Act 1986, section 214, see paragraph 11.23, below).

Directors may also be made directly liable to creditors when the company is not being wound up:

(a) for breach of the restrictions on the re-use of company names (Insolvency Act 1986, section 217, see paragraph 11.24, below).

(b) for acting while disqualified (Company Directors Disqualification Act 1986, section 15, see paragraph 1.30 ff, above).

In these circumstances the director's liability is joint and several with the company itself and any other person who is liable in the same way. A creditor may take direct action for recovery without the intervention of a liquidator or a government agency. Such actions enable the creditor to recover in full for his own benefit.

Directors can be made personally liable if the company is liable to civil penalties for VAT evasion involving dishonesty under section 13 of the Finance Act 1985. A penalty equal to the amount of tax evaded can be applied under this section irrespective of whether criminal liability has been incurred. Where it appears that the conduct giving rise to the penalty is in any way attributable to a director the penalty may be levied on the director instead of the company, or apportioned between them (Finance Act 1986, section 14). These provisions apply whether or not the company is in liquidation.

11.21 Misfeasance and breach of duty

An officer of the company may be ordered to compensate it if, in the course of a winding up, it appears that he has misappropriated its money or property or been guilty of any misfeasance or breach of duty to it (Insolvency Act 1986, section 212). (An order may also be made in respect of anyone who has acted as an insolvency practitioner in relation to the company, or anyone who has been concerned in its promotion, formation or management.) Application for the order may be made by the official receiver, the liquidator, a creditor or (with the court's permission) a shareholder (Insolvency Act 1986, section 212).

Misfeasance generally means the improper performance by an officer of something which he has a duty to perform properly. However, in the context of section 212 it does not apply to all examples of misconduct but only to those which result in actual loss to the company (*Re Derek Randall Enterprises Ltd* [1990] BCC 749). The section is concerned only with compensating the company and does not extend a director's liability for breach of duty.

11.22 Fraudulent trading

If it appears that the business of the company has been carried on with the intention of defrauding creditors or for any other fraudulent purpose, anyone knowingly a party to the carrying on of the business in that manner:

(a) can be held liable to make such contributions to the company's assets as the court thinks proper (Insolvency Act 1986, section 213); and

(b) is liable to imprisonment or a fine, or both (Companies Act 1985, section 458).

In *Re a Company No 001418 of 1988* [1990] BCC 526 it was held that the compensatory sum for which the respondent was liable was the trading loss during the period of fraudulent trading. An additional punitive element was also considered appropriate.

The civil remedy imposing personal liability can only be obtained on application by the liquidator in the course of a winding up. However, the criminal offence can be committed irrespective of whether the company is being wound up.

The interrelationship between the civil and criminal provisions under the Companies Act has provoked difficulties in obtaining redress in the past. In practice, it was often necessary to establish guilty intention in civil cases to the standard of proof required by criminal law. However, the wrongful trading provisions of the Insolvency Act 1986 may go some way towards solving this problem by offering an alternative remedy (see paragraph 11.23, below).

As for what constitutes fraudulent trading, the courts have been reluctant to put forward a definition and it is difficult to formulate general principles from the decided cases. It is clearly fraud for a person who knows that he cannot pay for goods to induce a supplier to deliver them (*Re Gerald Cooper Chemicals Ltd* [1978] Ch 262; *R v Grantham* [1984] QB 675). The prospect of non-payment need only be reasonably certain:

> 'if a company continues to carry on business and to incur debts at a time when there is, to the knowledge of the directors, no reasonable prospect of the creditors ever receiving payment of those debts, it is, in general, a proper inference that the company is carrying on business with intent to defraud'.

(*Re William C Leitch Bros Ltd* [1932] 2 Ch 71.)

However, a subsequent civil case narrowed this finding by holding that there must be 'real dishonesty, involving, according to current notions of fair trading among commercial men at the present day, real moral blame' (*Re Patrick & Lyon Ltd* [1933] Ch 786). It has also been held that there can be no criminal conviction for fraudulent trading unless dishonesty has been proved (*R v Cox and Hodges* (1982) 75 Cr App Rep 291). In *R v Grantham* [1984] QB 675 the Court of Appeal suggested that the court is entitled to find dishonesty if a person obtains credit when he knows that there is no good reason for thinking that funds will become available to pay the debt when it becomes due or shortly thereafter.

Mere failure to act has been held not to constitute fraudulent trading. In *Re Maidstone Buildings Provisions Ltd* [1971] 3 All ER 363 the company secretary (who was also financial adviser) failed to inform the directors that the company was trading while insolvent, but the failure to give advice was held to be insufficient to make him liable for carrying on the company's business while insolvent.

11.23 Wrongful trading

In addition to the existing provisions regarding fraudulent trading, the Insolvency Act 1985 introduced the new concept of personal liability for wrongful trading (Insolvency Act 1986, section 214). Unlike fraudulent trading, wrongful trading is not also a criminal offence and the burden of proof required to impose liability should therefore be one based on a balance of probabilities rather than on the criminal standard of 'beyond reasonable doubt'. In practice, therefore, directors – including shadow directors – are likely to face an increased risk of personal liability for the company's debts, and of consequent disqualification.

On application by the liquidator, the court may make an order declaring that a person is liable to make a contribution to the company's assets if:

(a) the company has gone into insolvent liquidation (that is, its assets are insufficient to meet its debts and other liabilities and to pay for the costs of liquidation);

(b) at some time before the commencement of the winding up the person knew or ought to have concluded that there was no reasonable prospect of the company avoiding insolvent liquidation;

(c) he was a director or shadow director at that time;

(d) the court is satisfied that the director did not take every step he ought to have taken to minimise the potential loss to creditors.

In determining what the director should have known and done, the court will expect reasonable diligence on his part and also take into account both:

(a) the general knowledge, skill and experience that might reasonably be expected of someone carrying out his function within the company; and

(b) the general knowledge, skill and experience that he actually has.

The effect of all this is that a director (or shadow director) is required to recognise the moment when his company can no longer avoid insolvent liquidation and to take immediate and positive action to protect the interests of creditors. In doing so he will be required to display an objective level of skill. So if he has a designated function within the company he will be expected to possess the skills appropriate to carrying out that function competently and to apply them diligently. He will be expected to act not merely as a reasonable man, but as a skilled director.

These provisions are not just aimed at rogue directors. They can also catch misguided directors who attempt to trade their way out of a hopeless situation and directors whose inattention or lack of acumen leaves them unaware of the company's true position.

Some directors will be more at risk than others. Since the tests for insolvency are finance related, the finance director, or any director responsible for an accounting function, is particularly vulnerable, even if he relies on bookkeeping staff to carry out the work. Similarly, a director with a finance related qualification faces an increased risk, even if his executive duties include no direct accounting responsibilities. The managing director also, because of his function, will probably be expected to display a higher standard of skill.

The position of a non-executive director will probably depend on his precise role in the organisation and his background, but he cannot expect to avoid responsibility merely because he is not involved in day-to-day management. Indeed, the monitoring role commonly assumed by a non-executive director could result in a significant responsibility in the event of a failure.

To protect himself, each director should ensure that his function is clearly and accurately defined, so as to avoid any misunderstanding about the extent of his responsibilities. He should not take on any duties for which he is not adequately equipped. To minimise his risk of liability, each director should keep himself fully informed as to the company's cash and trading profiles, and take a realistic view of the company's future prospects. A checklist of the sort of management information required is given in Appendix VII.

Once a director has concluded that insolvent liquidation is inevitable he has the task of convincing his colleagues on the board. If he is unable to do so he is in a difficult position since the steps to be taken normally require the directors to act together as a board. Some of the alternatives open to a dissenting director are discussed in paragraph 8.20, above. When faced with insolvent liquidation, the board should normally seek specialist professional advice for an expert assessment of the options. These include:

(a) selling the business as a going concern;

(b) a voluntary arrangement with creditors;

(c) the appointment by a secured creditor of an administrative receiver;

(d) the appointment of an administrator to manage the company on behalf of all the creditors;

(e) a creditors' voluntary winding up (that is, a voluntary winding up in which the directors cannot make a statutory declaration of solvency).

If the court makes an order against a director for wrongful trading it may also make a disqualification order (see paragraph 1.34, above).

The first wrongful trading case to be reported was *Re Produce Marketing Consortium Ltd* (1989) 5 BCC 569 which made a number of important points. The court's discretion under section 214 of the Insolvency Act 1986 was compensatory rather than penal. There need be no fraudulent intent on the part of the directors. While the level of expertise required of a director would depend upon the size of the company and business, and the sophistication of the accounting procedures, there were certain minimum standards that are assumed to have been attained. The knowledge to be imputed to a director was not limited to the facts that a director ought to know but also those that he ought to ascertain.

In *Re DKG Contractors Ltd* [1990] BCC 903 the court ordered that under the wrongful trading provisions the compensation should be assessed as the sum of the trade debts incurred by the company on or after the date wrongful trading was found to have commenced.

11.24 Restriction on the re-use of company names

Directors of a company which goes into insolvent liquidation are prohibited for five years from trading through a company or business of the same or a similar name (Insolvency Act 1986, section 216). The restriction applies to anyone who was a director or shadow director at any time during the 12 months prior to the liquidation. Breach of the rules is a criminal offence.

In addition, anyone involved in the management of a company which uses a prohibited name may be personally liable for the company's debts (Insolvency Act 1986, section 217). This liability extends to anyone involved in the management of the company who acts on instructions given (without the leave of the court) by a person prohibited from using the name.

These provisions are designed primarily to prevent directors defaulting on obligations to creditors of one company but immediately setting up a 'phoenix' company of a similar name to carry on the business, often with the old company's assets obtained at forced sale prices. There are certain prescribed exceptions to the rules, designed to make it possible for an insolvency practitioner to realise the goodwill contained in the name. The court may also make exceptions.

11.30 VOIDABLE TRANSACTIONS AND TRANSACTIONS DEFRAUDING CREDITORS

The provisions of the Companies Act relating to fraudulent transfers and preferences were replaced in the Insolvency Act 1985 with a new range of provisions dealing with:

(a) transactions at an undervalue (Insolvency Act 1986, section 238);

(b) 'voidable' preferences (Insolvency Act 1986, section 239);

(c) transactions defrauding creditors (Insolvency Act 1986, sections 423 to 425).

The court has wide powers under these rules to restore the parties to their former position provided it does not prejudice the rights of innocent third parties. In addition, disqualification may be imposed in respect of transactions defrauding creditors (dealt with in paragraph 11.33, below).

11.31 Transactions at an undervalue

A transaction at an undervalue occurs where the company confers a benefit without obtaining adequate consideration, at a time when it is unable to pay its debts (Insolvency Act 1986, section 238). If the transaction is with a connected person such as a director the onus is on that person to show that the company was not insolvent at the time. The court has power to reverse such a transaction if it took place in the two years before the company went into liquidation, unless it was made in good faith for the carrying on of the business in the reasonable belief that the company would benefit.

11.32 Preferences

The court can also set aside transactions which would improve the position of a particular creditor in a liquidation, provided the company was influenced by a desire to bring about such an improvement (Insolvency Act 1986, section 239). Such preferences are voidable if made at a time when the company was insolvent and in the six months prior to a liquidation. However, this period is extended to two years (although not in Scotland) if the preference is in favour of a connected person, in which case there is also a presumption that the company was both insolvent and influenced by a desire to improve the connected person's position in the event of a liquidation.

The first case to be reported under this section was *Re M C Bacon Ltd* [1990] BCC 78. In this case the liquidator was seeking to set aside a debenture granted to a bank. It was held that the mere presence of a desire to improve a creditor's position was not enough. The desire must have influenced the decision to enter into the transaction. In this instance it was decided that the directors were only motivated by the desire to avoid the overdraft being called in and to continue trading and the liquidator's application was dismissed. It should be noted that this case did not relate to a connected person so there was no presumption of influence (see above). It was also stated that cases decided before the Insolvency Act 1986 were irrelevant to an interpretation of section 239 given the complete and deliberate change of language.

11.33 Transactions defrauding creditors

Transactions at an undervalue made for the purpose of putting assets beyond the reach of creditors are regarded as transactions defrauding creditors. The court has the power to set aside such transactions and restore the position of the parties, subject to protecting the rights of innocent third parties. Application for the exercise of this power may be made by an insolvency practitioner administering the company or by the victim of such a transaction (Insolvency Act 1986, section 424). Directors responsible for such transactions may be adjudged unfit to hold office and disqualified (see paragraph 1.33, above).

In specifying these provisions against debt avoidance the Act does not in any way exclude directors from liability for fraud and other wrongful acts under other statutes.

Appendix I

Summary of minority rights under the Companies Act 1985

Minority required	*Right available*	*Section*
Any member	To apply to the court for an order on the ground that the company's business is being conducted in a manner which is unfairly prejudicial to the interests of its members generally or some part of its members.	459 (see paragraph 7.44, above)
Any member	To apply to the court for cancellation of a special resolution approving any payment out of capital for the redemption or purchase of a private company's own shares.	176 (see paragraph 6.22, above)
5% of issued share capital; or 50 members	To apply to the court for cancellation of a special resolution by a public company to re-register as a private company.	54
5% (of the voting rights); or not less than 100 members representing an average £100 each of shares	To requisition the circulation of resolutions and notices.	376
10% of paid up voting capital	To require the company to exercise its powers under section 212 to investigate interests in its voting shares.	214

Minority required	*Right available*	*Section*
10% of the paid up voting capital	To requisition an extraordinary general meeting, notwithstanding anything in the company's articles.	368 (see paragraph 7.12, above)
10% of the paid up voting capital, or 10% of the total voting rights; or 5 members	To demand a poll at a general meeting (any provision in the articles excluding this right is void).	373 (see paragraph 7.20, above)
10% of the issued shares; or 200 members	To apply to the Secretary of State for the appointment of inspectors to investigate the company's affairs.	431 (see paragraph 4.71, above)
10% of the issued shares; or 200 members	To apply to the Secretary of State to investigate the ownership of the company	442 (see paragraph 4.73, above)
Any holder of shares that are part of a 10% or smaller minority after a take-over	To compel the acquirer of 90% or more of the company's shares under a take-over offer to acquire a minority shareholding.	430A (see paragraph 6.50, above)
15% of issued capital (or any class thereof)	To apply to the court for cancellation of an alteration of the company's objects.	5

Minority required	*Right available*	*Section*
15% of issued capital (or any class thereof)	To apply to the court for cancellation of an alteration of conditions in the memorandum that could lawfully have been in the articles.	17
15% of shares of relevant class	To apply to the court for cancellation of an alteration of class rights where the alteration is unfairly prejudicial.	127

In addition, the following majorities are required for certain procedures, giving minorities an effective blocking power.

100%	To pass an elective resolution.	379A (see paragraph 7.30, above)
100%	To pass a written resolution.	381A (see paragraph 7.32, above)
100%	To call an annual general meeting at short notice.	369 (see paragraph 7.14, above)
95%	To call an extraordinary general meeting at short notice.	369 (see paragraph 7.14, above)
95%	To accept less than 21 days' notice of a general meeting at which a special resolution is to be proposed.	378
75%	To pass a special or an extraordinary resolution.	378 (see paragraph 7.30, above)

Appendix II

Changes in accounting reference period

Changes can only be made in the accounting reference period in accordance with the rules shown in the table.

Change	*Change notified in respect of*	
	Current period	
1 Which lengthens the period	Only if the new ARD is that of its parent undertaking or its subsidiary undertaking and the time limit for filing the previous financial statements has not expired (section 225(5)). The ARP must not exceed 18 months (section 225(6)).	Only if: (a) no earlier extension of an ARP has been made by the company; or (b) at least five years have passed from the end of any earlier ARP which itself had been extended; or (c) the new ARD is that of its parent undertaking or its subsidiary undertaking (section 225(4)). The ARP must not exceed eighteen months (section 225(6)).
2 Which shortens the period	Only if the new ARD is that of its parent undertaking or its subsidiary undertaking and the time limit for filing the previous financial statements has not expired (section 225(5)).	No restrictions

ARD = Accounting reference date
ARP = Accounting reference period

Appendix III

Directors' interests in shares

The following table summarises the specific rules for determining the interests which are included in and excluded from the disclosure requirements (see paragraph 4.31, above).

Included	*Excluded*
(i) An interest as a beneficiary under a trust (Schedule 13, paragraph 2).	(i) A person holding as a bare trustee or custodian trustee (Schedule 13, paragraph 10).
(ii) Joint interests (each notifiable) (Schedule 13, paragraph 7).	(ii) Interests arising as a trustee or personal representative where the Public Trustee is also a trustee or personal representative (SI 1985/802).
(iii) An interest arising from a contract for the purchase of shares or debentures (Schedule 13, paragraph 3).	(iii) A remainder interest in trust property, so long as the life interest subsists (Schedule 13, paragraph 9).
(iv) An entitlement to exercise any right conferred by the holding of shares or debentures (except as holder of a proxy for a specified meeting) (Schedule 13, paragraph 3).	(iv) Interests of a director of a reporting company, which is a wholly-owned subsidiary, and the director is also the director of the parent company which will report the interest (SI 1985/802).
(v) A right to call for delivery of shares or debentures, a right to acquire an interest and an obligation to take an interest in shares or debentures (Schedule 13, paragraph 6). (A right to subscribe does not constitute an interest for these purposes (Schedule 13, paragraph 6), but must be disclosed in its own right (see paragraph 4.31, above).	(v) Where a company is a wholly-owned subsidiary of a company incorporated outside Great Britain, interests in any group companies incorporated outside Great Britain (SI 1985/802).

Included	*Excluded*
(vi) An interest acquired through another company, if that company is interested and (a) that company or its directors are accustomed to act in accordance with the instructions of the notifying director; or (b) the notifying director controls one-third of the voting power in that company (Schedule 13, paragraph 4).	(vi) Interests in shares arising solely on account of a limitation in the memorandum or articles on a person's rights of disposal of shares (SI 1985/802). (vii) Interests in shares or debentures of a society registered under the Industrial and Provident Societies Act 1965 (SI 1985/802). (viii) Interests as a trustee or beneficiary of an approved superannuation fund or retirement benefit scheme (SI 1985/802).

Bare trustee – A trustee with no duties except to convey the assets to or by the direction of the beneficiaries. He should have no beneficial interest in the context of these rules (eg a nominee).

Custodian trustee – A trustee in whose name assets have been vested but who has no powers of administration. He is bound to act in accordance with the directions of the managing trustees as long as there is no breach of trust (eg a bank which holds the assets of a unit trust).

Appendix IV

Table of permitted transactions concerning directors

(under the Companies Act 1985, sections 332 to 338)

Transactions, agreements, arrangements and guarantees between a company (or its subsidiary) and a director of the company (or a person connected with the director) in relation to loans, quasi-loans and credit transactions are generally prohibited, except as noted below. (Other transactions etc are generally permitted, except that special rules apply to directors' service contracts (section 319) and substantial transfers of non-cash assets between companies and directors (section 320).)

Loans, quasi-loans and credit transactions which are permitted are:

Permitted for	*Loans*	*Quasi-loans*	*Credit transactions*
1 Any company	A company may make a loan to a director if the aggregate amount does not exceed £5,000 (section 334). A company may provide a director with funds (up to £20,000 in the case of a public company) to meet expenditure for the purposes of the company or to enable him to perform his duties. Approval of the company in general meeting is required, failing which the loan etc is repayable within six months (section 337).		
2 Public company or member of a group which includes a public company ('relevant company')	Not permitted (except as above).	Only if reimbursible within two months, and the total for the director does not exceed £5,000 (section 332).	Either (i) where transaction is under normal commercial terms; Or (ii) where the total for the director does not exceed £10,000 (section 335).

Permitted for:	*Loans*	*Quasi-loans*	*Credit transactions*
3 Private company not a member of a group which includes a public company	Not permitted to a director (except as above). May be made to a connected person.	Permitted.	Permitted.
4 Money-lending company	Either (i) where loan etc is under normal commercial terms, with upper limit of £100,000 per director (no upper limit for a recognised bank or for a private company not the subsidiary or a public company); Or (ii) where loan etc is on terms available to other employees and is in connection with the purchase or improvement of the director's main residence, with an upper limit of £100,000 per director (section 338).		No special rules.

Notes:

1 Definitions may be found in the Act of the terms 'quasi-loans' and 'credit transactions' (section 331), 'money-lending company' (section 338), 'relevant amount' (section 339), and 'value' of transaction and arrangements (section 340).

2 'Director' includes 'shadow director' – that is, one on whose instructions the directors are accustomed to act (excluding professional advice).

3 Other minor exemptions may be found in sections 333 and 336.

Appendix V

Table of disclosures of transactions concerning directors

(as required by the Companies Act 1985, section 232 and Sch 6, Part II)

The particulars indicated by the table below should be disclosed by way of notes to the accounts in relation to each transaction, agreement, arrangement or guarantee (or security given) whether permitted or not between a company (or its subsidiary) and a director of the company (or a person connected with the director) in respect of loans, quasi-loans, credit transactions and other transactions. Directors include shadow directors. Corresponding amounts are not required.

Note: There are specific exemptions relating to banking companies and a number of further minor exemptions which are not covered by the table below.

Particulars to be disclosed	*Loans*	*Quasi-loans*	*Credit transactions*	*Other material transactions except service contracts**
1 The principal terms of the transaction etc including: 2 a statement that the transaction etc was made or subsisted during the year; 3 the name of the director (and, where applicable, the connected person);	Yes.	Yes.	Yes – except where the aggregate outstanding sum for a director did not exceed £5,000 during the financial year.	Yes – except where the aggregate interest in each transaction with a director did not exceed either: (i) the lower of £5,000 and 1% of net asset value or (ii) £1,000 during the financial year.

Particulars to be disclosed – contd	*Loans – contd*	*Quasi-loans – contd*	*Credit transactions – contd*	*Other material transactions except service contracts* – contd*
4 the nature of his interest in the transaction;	N/A	N/A	N/A	Yes – except as above.
5 the amount due (including interest at the beginning and end of the financial year); 6 the maximum amount due during the financial year; 7 the amount of unpaid interest; 8 the amount of any provision;	Yes.	No – but see 9 below.	No.	No.
9 the value of the transactions etc;	No (but see 5–8 above).	Yes.	Yes – except as above.	Yes – except as above.
And in the case of a guarantee (or security): 10 the amounts guaranteed (secured) at the beginning and end of the financial year; 11 the maximum liability guaranteed (secured); and 12 any amount paid or incurred since the inception of the guarantee (security).	Yes.	Yes.	Yes – except as above.	No.

If the financial statements do not give this information the auditor must give it in his report (section 237 (4)).

* A material transaction is one where the director's interest is material in the opinion of the majority of the other directors.

Appendix VI

Contents of directors' report

The directors' report must contain the following information.

(a) *Principal activities* The report must state the principal activities during the financial year and details of any significant changes.

(b) *Review of developments* The directors must provide 'a fair review' of the development of the business during the financial year and of the position at the end of it. What constitutes a fair review is to be determined by the directors.

(c) *Future developments* The report must contain an indication of likely future developments in the business.

(d) *Research and development* The report must contain an indication of the activities (if any) of the company and its subsidiaries in the field of research and development.

(e) *Dividends and reserves* The report must state the amount, if any, recommended to be paid as dividend and the amount to be transferred to reserves. Where the directors do not propose a dividend it is customary to state this.

(f) *Post-balance sheet events* Particulars must be given of any important events affecting the company (or any of its subsidiaries) which have occurred since the end of the financial year.

(g) *Fixed assets* The report must contain particulars of any significant changes in fixed assets during the year. It must also disclose any substantial difference between the market value and balance sheet value of interests in land if the directors consider this is significant to members or debenture holders.

(h) *Acquisition of own shares* Where a company acquires its own shares during the year it must disclose certain information, including:

(i) the number and nominal value of shares purchased and the percentage of the called up share capital which those shares represent;

(ii) the consideration paid; and

(iii) the reason for the purchase.

(i) *Directors' names* Disclosure is required of the names of the persons who were directors of the company during the year. The following information is also often given, although it is not specifically required:

(i) the dates of appointments or resignations occurring during the period;

(ii) changes in the composition of the board after the year end;

(iii) the directors who retire at the annual general meeting, and whether they offer themselves for re-election;

(iv) the citizenship of non-UK directors.

(j) *Directors' interests in shares or debentures* (see paragraph 4.31, above).

(k) *Directors' interests in share/debenture options exercised or granted* (see paragraph 4.31, above).

(l) *Health and safety at work* Schedule 7, paragraph 10 requires certain companies (to be prescribed by the Secretary of State) to disclose in the directors' report such information as may be prescribed about arrangements for securing the health, safety and welfare of employees at work and for protecting others against risks to health and safety. No regulations have yet been prescribed.

(m) *Disabled persons* The report of a company with more than 250 employees (companies in groups do not have to aggregate their employees for this purpose) must describe the company's policy for the recruitment, continued employment and training and career development of disabled persons.

(n) *Employee involvement* The report of a company with more than 250 employees (companies in groups do not have to aggregate their employees for this purpose) must contain certain information about how the company informs and consults employees about matters of concern to them, and how it aims to encourage the involvement of employees in the company's performance.

(o) *Political and charitable gifts* If a company and its subsidiaries have given money for political or charitable purposes (or both) amounting to more than £200, then the amount given in each category must be disclosed; the recipient of a political donation of over £200 must be named and the amount disclosed.

(p) *Insurance for officers and auditors* The report must state the fact if the company has purchased or maintained during the financial year any insurance to indemnify any officer or auditor against liability incurred by him in relation to the company.

(q) *Auditors* Although there is no statutory requirement for the directors' report to refer to the re-appointment of the auditor, it is normal for it to do so.

(r) *Listed companies* The Stock Exchange requires certain additional information from listed companies, which is usually included in the directors' report:

(i) geographical analysis of turnover and results;

(ii) an explanation of significant differences between the results shown in the accounts and any forecast made;

(iii) certain additional information concerning arrangements for the company to acquire its own shares;

(iv) changes in the interests of directors in shares and debentures since the year end;

(v) the unexpired period of the service contract of any director proposed for re-election;

(vi) substantial holdings of the company's shares;

(vii) directors' material interests in contracts with the company;

(viii) contracts with corporate substantial shareholders;

(ix) whether or not the company is a close company for tax purposes;

(x) particulars of any agreement to waive dividends.

Appendix VII

Checklist of directors' responsibilities in relation to unfitness and wrongful trading

This checklist sets out some of the matters which insolvency practitioners, the Department of Trade and Industry and the courts will take into account when considering directors' responsibilities. It is based on the provisions of the Insolvency Act and the Department of Trade and Industry publication entitled 'Guidance Notes – Disqualification of Directors: Completion of Statutory Reports and Returns'. It is not exhaustive and it does not cover technical responsibilities after formal insolvency procedures have begun. However, it does set out some guidelines for directors to follow in properly conducting their management of the company.

UNFITNESS

Breach of duty to company

Are you clear that you have not received any reward from the company (other than by way of agreed remuneration or dividends) which had the effect of diminishing its capital base?

Can you confirm that you have never been the means whereby anyone else has received such a reward?

Can you confirm that you have not been party to the disposal of assets of the company to its detriment?

Are you certain that you have not retained or failed to account for property of the company, or applied it other than in furtherance of its business?

Have you fully disclosed to the company any transactions affecting its assets which have caused (or may cause) the company loss?

Have you fully and formally disclosed to the company any personal or conflicting interest you have had in its dealings?

When you have been party to the disposal of company assets, has the consideration always been adequate?

Breach of duty to creditors

Can you confirm that you have never taken steps in an attempt to place any of the company's assets beyond the reach of its creditors?

Can the company trade without relying on receiving deposits or prepayments from consumer customers?

If you receive deposits from consumers, is the company performing its obligations to the customer within a reasonable period?

Are you satisfied that all consumer customers who have made prepayments will receive the goods or services they have ordered or that there are adequate measures available to ensure they are repaid in full?

Are you satisfied that no statement has been made to any creditor which could be regarded as misleading?

Annual accounts, audit and statutory returns

Has the company complied with its statutory reporting requirements as regards audited accounts?

Have you given all qualifications in audit reports due consideration, and ensured that appropriate action has been taken?

Has the appropriate action similarly been taken on all significant shortcomings raised in audit management letters?

Are you up-to-date with filing your Annual Returns? (filed within 28 days of the return date)

Have audited accounts been filed? (not later than seven months after the year end for plcs and ten months for private companies)

Have all statutory notices been filed up-to-date? (eg appointments and resignations of directors and secretaries, change of registered office, registration or satisfaction of mortgages, increases or issues of shares, special resolutions, etc)

Statutory books and accounting records

Is the minute book complete and up-to-date?

Does it fully reflect all significant matters considered and decisions taken by the board?

Are the company's registers of shareholders and of directors and their interests complete and up-to-date?

Do the company's accounting records adequately reflect the conduct of the business and are they kept up-to-date?

Have you ensured that the company's records are retained for at least the minimum period (three years for private, or six for public, companies)?

If any accounting records are kept overseas, are returns regularly received and available for inspection in this country?

WRONGFUL TRADING

Management accounts

Do you receive a monthly management accounts package on a timely basis?

Does this package adequately explain to you the company's present financial position?

Is the package properly prepared by the company's accounting staff and reviewed by the financial director?

Are variances from budget adequately explained and the consequences highlighted?

Budgets and forecasts

Are trading and cash flow projections regularly prepared for a period of at least twelve months forward on a proper basis?

Are these forecasts monitored against actual performance, and are variances explained and consequences reviewed?

Cash management

Are the company's present and projected financial requirements, as shown by the management accounts, within agreed bank and loan facilities?

Could your company pay its suppliers within the contractual periods of credit without exceeding agreed banking facilities?

Do the company's existing banking facilities permit the payment on the due dates of amounts owing in respect of PAYE, National Insurance and VAT?

Can you confirm that the company's bankers have indicated no intention to curtail its facilities?

Do you regularly review the likelihood that any contingent or prospective liability of the company may become actual?

Can you confirm that none is likely to do so within the next twelve months?

If any contingent liability becomes actual, will the company have adequate finance to meet it?

If your company is in financial difficulties

If the company continues to trade, can it avoid insolvent liquidation?

Have you taken advice on the options available?

Appendix VIII

Model code for securities – Transactions by directors of listed companies

Reproduced by kind permission of the Council of the Stock Exchange.

The Council regards it as highly desirable that directors of listed companies should hold securities in their own companies. Directors wishing to buy or sell such securities must first have regard to the statutory provisions in the Company Securities (Insider Dealing) Act 1985 on insider dealing. It is regarded as axiomatic that directors of listed companies will not deal in their companies' securities when prohibited from doing so by those statutory provisions. The statutory provisions are not confined to directors of listed companies but concern themselves more widely with individuals 'connected with a company'.

The Council believes that special considerations apply to directors of listed companies. There are occasions where, even though not expressly prohibited by the statutory provisions, it would be undesirable for a director to buy or sell his company's securities.

These occasions are:

(i) where a director is himself unaware of a price-sensitive matter under discussion (perhaps because it has not yet been made known to the board) which is likely ultimately to call for an exceptional announcement and where for his own protection he should be told not to deal; and

(ii) the periods prior to the regular announcements of results and dividends.

The purpose of the model code remains primarily to give guidance on these two occasions so as to enable companies to establish an agreed procedure which would provide general protection against misinformed criticism both for the company and for the individual directors, given that, under the statutory provisions, a director might otherwise be free to deal. The Council sees the model code (including the basic principles set out below) as setting a minimum standard of good practice against which companies should measure their own company codes. The model code should therefore be seen as setting guidelines rather than rigid rules to be followed in every detail.

Two further aspects should be mentioned:

(i) compliance with the model code is not a defence in law and it may therefore be necessary to be satisfied that a proposed dealing would not be in contravention of the statutory provisions. It should not, for example, be assumed that compliance with the procedure set out in basic principle 5 (to establish the time at which an intended acquisition by a company should be deemed price-sensitive information) or that dealing under the extenuating circumstances indicated in rule 3.1 (where a pressing financial commitment has to be met) would necessarily preclude contravention of the statutory provisions. Basic principle 5 and rule 3.1 are intended as guidance for the chairman (or whoever is nominated to receive notification of dealing intentions) as to circumstances where exceptions to the model code may be considered, always assuming that no breach of the statutory provisions would result; and

(ii) the statutory provisions do not specifically relate to other interests of a director, nor to the position of spouses or infant children. In this respect the model code has broader application than the statutory provisions.

The basic principles

1 Directors should not deal in their companies' securities on considerations of a short-term nature.

2 Directors will always be thought to be in possession of more information than can at any particular time be published. Accordingly they must accept that they cannot at all times feel free to deal in their companies' securities, even when the statutory provisions would not prohibit them from doing so.

3 Notwithstanding this general constraint there must be periods in the year when directors are in principle (but subject to the statutory provisions) to be regarded as free to deal in their companies' securities. The following model rules have been formulated on the basis that:

(i) dealings should not normally take place for a minimum period prior to the announcement of regularly recurring information, particularly profits, dividends and other distributions, whether or not the information is price-sensitive (this period being defined in rule 3.1); and

(ii) dealings should not take place prior to the announcement of matters of an exceptional nature involving unpublished price-sensitive information in relation to the market price of the securities of the company (or where relevant any other listed company).

4 For the purpose of the model code, the grant to a director of an option to subscribe or purchase his company's securities shall be regarded as a dealing by him, if the price at which such option may be exercised is fixed at the time of such grant. If, however, an option is granted to a director on terms whereby the price at which such option may be exercised is to be fixed at the time of exercise, the dealing is to be regarded as taking place at the time of exercise.

5 Matters of an exceptional nature cause particular difficulty. A director who has knowledge of the exceptional matter in question will normally be prohibited from dealing by the statutory provisions but even if he is not so prohibited he should nevertheless not deal in the circumstances outlined below. Similarly, a director who has no such knowledge should be advised, when he notifies his intention to deal under rule 2.1, that it would be inappropriate for him to deal where the same circumstances apply. Those circumstances are where:

(i) the matter in question constitutes unpublished price-sensitive information in relation to the company's securities; and

(ii) the proposed dealing would take place after the time when the likelihood of an announcement ultimately being necessary has become a reasonable probability.

An exhaustive definition of price-sensitive information is not possible. Nevertheless it should be assumed for this purpose that the matters referred to in paragraph 10 and paragraphs 14 to 19 inclusive of Chapter 2 of this Section are to be so regarded.

6 In principle, a director should seek to secure that all dealings in which he is or is deemed to be interested should be conducted in accordance with the provisions of the model code. Rule 4.1 sets this out as a general proposition. Nevertheless it is recognised that a director's duty in this respect will depend on the particular circumstances. A director who is sole trustee, for example, should

follow the same procedure as for any dealings on his own account and should deal only if he would be personally allowed to deal under the code, even if he is excepted from the general prohibitions imposed by the statutory provisions by virtue of the special defences relating to trustees granted by such provisions.

Where a director has co-trustees who are not themselves directors of the company, he may not be able to ensure that the procedure applicable to his personal dealings is followed in respect of dealings on behalf of the trust. The director/trustee has to avoid acting in breach of trust and at the same time to refrain from divulging or abusing confidential information, and it may not therefore always be practicable to expect that trustees will refrain from dealing at a time when one of their number is not personally free to deal.

On the other hand if a director, whether or not himself a trustee, has, as settlor or otherwise, an important influence over the decision of the trustees, the procedure applicable to his personal dealings ought to be followed and the trustees should not deal when he personally is not free to deal. Again, the remoteness of some interests may be such as to make the imposition of any duty under rule 4.1 impracticable or inappropriate. Rules 4.2 and 4.3 indicate certain precautions which should be taken.

It is an over-riding principle that under no circumstances should a director deal where prohibited from doing so by the statutory provisions or make any unauthorised disclosure of any confidential information, whether to co-trustees or any other person, or make any use of such information for the advantage of himself or others, even those to whom he owes a fiduciary duty.

7 When a director places investment funds under professional management, even where discretion is given, the managers should nonetheless be made subject to the same restrictions and procedures as the director himself in respect of proposed dealings in the company's securities.

The following model rules should be used as guidelines for companies in formulating their own codes:

1.1 A director should not deal in any of the securities of the company at any time when he is in possession of unpublished price-sensitive information in relation to those securities.

1.2 The same restrictions should apply to dealings by a director in the securities of any other listed company when by virtue of his position as a director of his own company, he is in possession of unpublished price-sensitive information in relation to those securities.

At other times, a director WHO IS NOT PROHIBITED FROM DOING SO BY THE COMPANY SECURITIES (INSIDER DEALING) ACT 1985 can feel free to deal subject to the provisions of the rules which follow:

2.1 A director should not deal in any securities of his own company without first notifying the chairman (or other director(s) appointed for the specific purpose), and receiving acknowledgement. In his own case the chairman should first notify the board at a board meeting, or alternatively notify the other director(s) appointed for the purpose and receive acknowledgement.

2.2 The procedure established within the company should, as a minimum, provide for there to be a written record maintained by the company that the appropriate notification was given and acknowledged, and for the director concerned to have written confirmation to that effect.

3.1 During the periods of two months immediately preceding the preliminary announcement of the company's annual results and of the announcement of the half-yearly results together with dividends and distributions to be paid or passed, a director should not purchase any securities of the company nor should he deal in securities in the circumstances set out in basic principle 5 above; nor should he sell any such securities unless the circumstances are exceptional, for example, where a pressing financial commitment has to be met. In any event he must comply with the procedure in rule 2 above.

3.2 Companies producing quarterly results should consult the Department on the formulation of modified dealing procedures appropriate to their case.

4.1 The restrictions on dealings by a director contained in this code should be regarded as equally applicable to any dealings by the director's spouse or by or on behalf of any infant child and any other dealings in which for the purposes of the Companies Act 1985 he is or is to be treated as interested. It is the duty of the director, therefore, to seek to avoid any such dealing at a time when he himself is not free to deal.

4.2 Any director of the company who acts as trustee of a trust should ensure that his co-trustees are aware of the identity of any company of which he is a director so as to enable them to anticipate possible difficulties. A director having funds under management should likewise advise the investment manager.

4.3 Any director who is a beneficiary, but not a trustee, of a trust which deals in securities of the company should endeavour to ensure that the trustees notify him after they have dealt in such securities on behalf of the trust, in order that he in turn may notify the company. For this purpose he should ensure that the trustees are aware of the companies of which he is a director.

5 A list of directors' dealings in the securities of the company since the date of the previous list should be circulated to members of the board with the board papers; alternatively the register maintained in accordance with section 325 of the Companies Act 1985 should be made available for inspection at every meeting of the board.

6 The directors of a company should as a board and individually endeavour to ensure that any employee of the company or director or employee of a subsidiary company who, because of his office or employment in the company or a subsidiary, is likely to be in possession of unpublished price-sensitive information in relation to the securities of any listed company, deals in those securities in accordance with this model code.

7 References in this code to 'securities' have the meanings ascribed thereto by section 12 of the Company Securities (Insider Dealing) Act 1985.

Appendix IX

Glossary

The following explanations are not intended to be strict legal definitions.

Accounting Standards Board (*ASB*) A body authorised to issue accounting standards for the purposes of the Act.

Administrator A person appointed by the court to manage a company in financial difficulties in order to protect creditors and, if possible, avoid liquidation. The administrator has the power to remove and appoint directors.

Agent Someone who is authorised to carry out business transactions on behalf of another (the principal) who is thereby bound by such actions.

Allotment The issue of shares.

Annual accounts The accounts which are prepared to fulfil the director's duty to present audited accounts to members in respect of each financial year. Annual accounts of limited companies must be filed with the registrar of companies. See also *Financial statements, Modified accounts.*

Annual general meeting A general meeting of the company's members which must be held in each calendar year within 15 months of the previous AGM. See also *General meeting, Extraordinary general meeting.*

Annual return A form filed each year with the registrar of companies containing specified information about the company's directors, shareholders, share capital etc.

Articles of association A constitutional document setting out the internal regulations of the company. Unless modified or excluded, the specimen articles in Table A have effect. See also *Table A.*

Audit The independent examination of, and expression of opinion on, the company's accounts. The auditor must be a chartered or certified accountant (or otherwise specifically authorised by the Department of Trade and Industry).

Authorised share capital See *Share capital.*

Board (*of directors*) See *Director*.

Calls See *Share*.

Capital See *Share capital*.

Case law The principles and rules of law established by judicial decisions. Under this system the decision reached in a particular case creates a precedent: that is, it is regarded as exemplifying rules of broader application which must be followed except by higher courts. See also *Common law*.

Certificate of incorporation A certificate issued by the registrar of companies on receipt of specified constitutional and other documents of the company. The company assumes its identity as a legal person on the date of certificate.

Charge A means by which a company offers its assets as security for a debt. A charge is a general term which includes, but is not limited to, a mortgage. A fixed charge relates to a specific asset or assets. A floating charge relates to whatever assets of a specified class are in the company's possession at the time the charge crystallises (if it does so).

Class rights The rights attached to different classes of shares.

Common law A body of law based on custom and usage and decisions reached in previous cases. The principles and rules of common law derive not from written legislation but from judgements and judicial opinions delivered in response to specific circumstances. See also *Case law, Statute law*.

Common seal A seal bearing a company's name for affixing to legal documents which are required to be under seal, such as deeds and share certificates. Depending on the articles, a director and the secretary usually have to add their signatures to the seal. The requirement that all companies must have a common seal was abolished by the Companies Act 1989 which also set out the procedures to be followed if documents are to have the same effect as if executed under seal.

Company An association of persons which, on incorporation, becomes a legal entity entirely separate from the individuals comprising its membership and which therefore continues unaffected by changes in membership. In the Companies Act 1985, 'company' is restricted to companies registered under that Act or previous Companies Acts. See also *Limited company, Private company, Public company, Unlimited company.*

Company secretary An officer of the company with a number of statutory duties, such as to sign the annual return and accompanying documents, and usually charged with a range of duties relating to the company's statutory books and records, filing requirements etc. Every company must have a secretary, who, in the case of a public company, must meet the qualification requirements laid down in the Act.

Contract An agreement between two or more persons creating a legally enforceable obligation between them.

Crime An offence against the Crown punishable by a fine or imprisonment or both.

Debenture A written acknowledgement of a debt owed by a company, often – but not necessarily – secured. It is common practice for a debenture to be created by a trust deed by which company property is mortgaged to trustees for the debenture holders, as security for the payment of interest and capital.

Department of Trade and Industry The government Department responsible for the administration of company law. The Companies Act confers certain powers on the Secretary of State for Trade and Industry.

Director An officer of the company responsible for determining policy, supervising the management of the company's business and exercising the powers of the company. Directors must generally carry out these functions collectively as a board.

Directors' report A statement attached to the annual accounts containing certain information laid down in the Act.

Distribution The transfer of some or all of a company's assets to its members, generally by way of dividend or on a winding up.

Dividends The distribution of a portion of the company's profits to members according to the class and amount of their shareholdings.

Elective resolution A resolution of which 21 days' notice must have been given requiring unanimous approval at a general meeting of a private company.

Extraordinary general meeting Any general meeting of the company's members that is not an annual general meeting. See also *Annual general meeting, General meeting.*

Extraordinary resolution A resolution requiring a 75% majority at a general meeting.

Fiduciary Having a position of trust, such that the power and authority conferred by the position must be exercised solely in the interests of the person with whom the fiduciary relationship exists. Trustees are in a fiduciary position, as are solicitors in relation to their clients. Directors have a fiduciary duty to the company, obliging them to act always in good faith and not to derive a personal profit from their position.

Financial Reporting Standards (FRSs) Accounting Standards issued by the Accounting Standards Board. Directors of companies, other than small or medium-sized companies, are required to disclose details of any non-compliance with applicable FRSs in their financial statements. See also *Accounting Standards Board.*

Financial statements The term adopted by the joint accountancy bodies to signify 'balance sheets, profit and loss accounts, statements of source and application of funds, notes and other statements which collectively are intended to give a true and fair view of financial position and profit or loss'. It is thus a description of the form and function of the annual accounts, for which term it is often substituted.

Financial year The period in respect of which the company's profits and loss account is drawn up; it need not coincide with the fiscal or calendar year and in certain circumstances need not be a year.

Floating charge See *Charge.*

General meeting A meeting of the company which all members are entitled to attend. The chief instrument of the general meeting is the resolution, by which members can by voting on a motion make their views known and, in some cases, enforce them. See also *Resolution.*

Guarantee A formal agreement under which a guarantor undertakes to be answerable for a contractual obligation of one person to another in the event of a default. A company limited by guarantee is one in which the liability of the members is limited to a specified amount in a winding up.

Insider dealing Buying or selling shares on the basis of an unfair advantage derived from access to price-sensitive information not generally available.

Intra vires Within the powers of the company as laid down in the objects clause of its memorandum of association. See also *Objects, Ultra vires.*

Limited company The commonest form of company, in which the liability of members for the debts of the company is limited – either to the amount of share capital for which they have applied (a company limited by shares) or to a specific amount guaranteed in the event of a winding up (a company limited by guarantee).

Liquidation The process under which a company ceases to trade and realises its assets for distribution to creditors and then shareholders. The term 'winding up' is synonymous.

Listed company A company whose shares are dealt on the Official List of The Stock Exchange.

Members The company's shareholders, of which there must be at least two.

Memorandum of association A constitutional document governing the company's relationship with the world at large, stating its name, domicile, objects, limitation of liability (if applicable) and authorised share capital.

Modified accounts A condensed version of the annual accounts which small and medium-sized companies (according to the specified size criteria) are allowed to file with the registrar of companies. They may not be used as a substitute for the full annual accounts for circulation to members. While the term is no longer used in the Act it has been retained in this publication for ease of reference. The

Auditing Guideline 'Reports by auditors – United Kingdom' uses the term 'abbreviated accounts' but states that there is nothing to preclude the use of the expression 'modified accounts'.

Nominal share capital See *Share capital.*

Objects The purposes for which the company was incorporated, as set out in the objects clause of its memorandum of association. In principle, a company cannot legally carry on activities outside the scope of its objects clause (but see *ultra vires*, below).

Office holder Under the Insolvency Act 1986, an insolvency practitioner acting as a company's liquidator, administrator or administrative receiver.

Officer Includes a director, manager or secretary of a company. Not everyone with the title of manager is sufficiently senior to be regarded as an officer, who must have a level of supervisory control which reflects the general policy of the company.

Ordinary resolution A resolution at a general meeting carried by a simple majority of votes actually cast.

Ordinary shares The most common form of share in a company, giving holders the right to share in the company's profits in proportion to their holdings and the right to vote at general meetings (although non-voting ordinary shares are occasionally encountered). See also *Share.*

Preference shares Shares carrying the right to payment of a fixed dividend out of profits before the payment of an ordinary dividend or the preferential return of capital or both. See also *Share.*

Private company A company that is not a public company.

Promoter A person engaged in setting up a company or in raising capital for a newly formed company. A person who acts merely as a professional adviser is not usually a promoter.

Prospectus Any prospectus, notice, circular, advertisement or other invitation to the public to subscribe for or purchase a company's shares or debentures.

Proxy A person authorised by a member to vote on his behalf at a general meeting.

Public company (plc) A company which meets specified requirements as to its minimum share capital and which is registered as a public company. Only public companies are allowed to offer their shares and debentures to the public.

Registered office The address at which legal documents may be served on the company and where the statutory books are normally kept. The registered office need not be the company's place of business and may be changed freely so long as it remains in the country of origin.

Registrar of companies The official responsible for maintaining the company records filed under the requirements of the Companies Act.

Resolution A decision at a meeting reached by a majority of members actually voting. See also *Elective resolution, Extraordinary resolution, Ordinary resolution, Special resolution, Written resolution.*

Seal See *Common seal.*

Secretary See *Company secretary.*

Share A unit of ownership of the company, representing a fraction of the share capital and usually conferring rights to participate in distributions. There may be several kinds of shares each carrying different rights. Shares are issued at a fixed nominal value, although the company may actually receive a larger amount, the excess representing share premium. Members may not be required to subscribe the full amount immediately, in which case the shares are partly paid. The members then await calls, which require them to pay further amounts until the shares are fully paid.

Share capital The capital of a company contributed or to be contributed by members. The authorised share capital is the maximum nominal amount the directors are authorised by the memorandum to issue. Issued, or allotted, share capital represents the amount actually contributed.

Share premium The excess of the price at which shares are issued above their nominal value.

Special resolution A resolution of which 21 days' notice has been given (although the period may be waived with the consent of 95% of the members) carried by at least 75% of the members actually voting at a general meeting.

Statement of source and application of funds (*Funds statement*) A financial statement showing how the company's operations have been financed and how its financial resources have been used during the financial year. Statement of Standard Accounting Practice No 10 requires a funds statement to be included with the annual accounts of most companies.

Statement of Standard Accounting Practice (*SSAP*) A statement by the joint accountancy bodies of rules which should be followed by members of those bodies when preparing accounts which are intended to show a true and fair view. The 22 SSAPs extant at 1 August 1990 were adopted by the Accounting Standards Board as Financial Reporting Standards. See also *Accounting Standards Board, Financial Reporting Standards.*

Statute law The body of law represented by legislation, and thus occurring in authoritative written form. Statute law contrasts with common law, over which it takes precedence.

Statutory books The general term applied to the registers etc that a company is required by the Companies Act to maintain.

Subscriber A person who subscribes to the memorandum of association and agrees to take up shares in the company.

Table A The specimen articles of association for a company limited by shares set out in the Companies (Tables A to F) Regulations 1985. Unless specifically modified or excluded, the version of Table A in force at the time of a company's incorporation automatically applies to the company. A significantly revised version of Table A was introduced on 1 July 1985, but companies incorporated earlier are not affected unless they specifically adopt its provisions.

Tort A breach of a legal duty that gives rise to a civil action for damages, such as negligence, trespass or libel.

Ultra vires Outside the powers set out in the company's constitution. Fundamental changes made by the Companies Act 1989 make the rule that a company cannot validly contract to do something outside the scope of the powers specifically granted in its memorandum, or that directors act *ultra vires* if they exceed their powers, largely a thing of the past (except for charitable companies). *Ultra vires* acts may be ratified by special resolution in certain circumstances, following changes made by the Companies Act 1989.

Unlimited company A company in which the members have unlimited liability for the company's debts in the event of a winding up.

Winding up See *Liquidation*.

Written resolution Allows private companies to move any resolution without holding a general meeting. The written resolution must be signed by all members who would have been able to vote.

Yellow Book *The Admission of Securities to Listing* published by The Stock Exchange which details the requirements which must be met by companies before their shares can be dealt on the Official List of The Stock Exchange.

For the full requirements, readers should refer to and rely only on the latest edition, available from the offices of the Council of The Stock Exchange.

Index

TOUCHE ROSS OFFICES IN THE UNITED KINGDOM, CHANNEL ISLANDS AND ISLE OF MAN

Aberdeen
66 Queen's Road, Aberdeen AB1 6YE
Telephone: 0224 325375 Fax: 0224 313611

Belfast
19 Bedford Street, Belfast BT2 7EJ
Telephone: 0232 322861 Fax: 0232 234786

Birmingham
Kensington House, 136 Suffolk Street Queensway, Birmingham B1 1LL
Telephone: 021 631 2288 Fax: 021 631 4512

Newater House, 11 Newhall Street, Birmingham B3 3NY
Telephone: 021 631 2288 Fax: 021 236 1513

Bournemouth
Richmond Point, 43 Richmond Hill, Bournemouth BH2 6LR
Telephone: 0202 291655 Fax: 0202 553551

Bracknell
Columbia Centre, Market Street, Bracknell, Berks RG12 1PA
Telephone: 0344 54445 Fax: 0344 422681

Bristol
Queen Anne House, 69–71 Queen Square, Bristol BS1 4JP
Telephone: 0272 211622 Fax: 0272 292801

Cambridge
Leda House, Station Road, Cambridge CB1 2RN
Telephone: 0223 460222 Fax: 0223 350839

Cardiff
Blenheim House, Fitzalan Court, Newport Road, Cardiff CF2 1TS
Telephone: 0222 481111 Fax: 0222 482615

Coleraine
Ferguson House, 23–25 Queen Street, Coleraine, Co Londonderry, Northern Ireland BT52 1BG
Telephone: 0265 51100 Fax: 0265 58286

Crawley
The Corn Exchange, 63 High Street, Crawley, West Sussex RH10 1BQ
Telephone: 0293 510112 Fax: 0293 533493

Dartford
Cornwallis House, Instone Road, Dartford DA1 2AG
Telephone: 0322 277777 Fax: 0322 291443

Edinburgh
8 Melville Crescent, Edinburgh EH3 7PQ
Telephone: 031 225 6834 Fax: 031 225 4049

6 Rutland Square, Edinburgh EH1 2AU
Telephone: 031 229 2208 Fax: 031 229 0842

Glasgow
39 St Vincent Place, Glasgow G1 2QQ
Telephone: 041 204 2800 Fax: 041 229 0842

65 Renfield Street, Glasgow G2 1NS
Telephone: 041 331 1501 Fax: 041 332 5038

Leeds
Eleven Albion Street, Leeds LS1 5PJ
Telephone: 0532 444741 Fax: 0532 435744

10–12 East Parade, Leeds LS1 2AJ
Telephone: 0532 439021 Fax: 0532 445580

Leicester
St John's House, East Street, Leicester LE1 6NG
Telephone: 0533 543598 Fax: 0533 552055

Liverpool
Reliance House, 20 Water Street, Liverpool L2 8UY
Telephone: 051 236 0941 Fax: 051 236 2877

London
Hill House, 1 Little New Street, London EC4A 3TR
Telephone: 071 936 3000 Fax: 071 583 8517

Friary Court, 65 Crutched Friars, London EC3N 2NP
Telephone: 071 936 3000 Fax: 071 480 6958

Peterborough Court, 133 Fleet Street, London EC4A 2TR
Telephone: 071 936 3000 Fax: 071 583 1198

Manchester
Abbey House, 74 Mosley Street, Manchester M60 2AT
Telephone: 061 228 3456 Fax: 061 228 2021

12 Booth Street, Manchester M60 2ED
Telephone: 061 228 3456 Fax: 061 228 2021

Milton Keynes
Ashton House, Silbury Boulevard, Central Milton Keynes
MK9 2HG
Telephone: 0908 666665 Fax: 0908 690510

Newcastle upon Tyne
Central Exchange Buildings, 93a Grey Street
Newcastle upon Tyne NE1 6EA
Telephone: 091 261 4111 Fax: 091 232 7665

Newport
14 Gold Tops, Newport, Gwent NP9 4UD
Telephone: 0633 251831 Fax: 0633 244458

Nottingham
1 Woodborough Road, Nottingham NG1 3FG
Telephone: 0602 500511 Fax: 0602 590060

Southampton
Carlton House, Carlton Place, Southampton SO1 2DZ
Telephone: 0703 334124 Fax: 0703 330724

Swansea
34 Orchard Street, Swansea SA1 5TS
Telephone: 0792 654182 Fax: 0792 655357

Isle of Man
Bank of Scotland House, Prospect Hill, Douglas, Isle of Man
Telephone: 0624 672332 Fax: 0624 672334

Guernsey
PO Box 137, Sydney Vane House, Rue du Commerce, St Peter Port
Guernsey, Channel Islands
Telephone: 0481 724011 Fax: 0481 711544

Jersey
P O Box 403, Lord Coutanche House, 66–68 Esplanade, St Helier,
Jersey, Channel Islands
Telephone: 0534 37770 Fax: 0534 34037